A to Z

bible
trivia

A to Z

bible trivia

the Ultimate Scripture Quiz

PAUL KENT

BARBOUR
PUBLISHING

Cover image © Chad J. Shaffer

Published by Barbour Publishing, Inc., P.O. Box 719,
Uhrichsville, Ohio 44683 www.barbourbooks.com

*Our mission is to publish and distribute inspirational products offering
exceptional value and biblical encouragement to the masses.*

Member of the
Evangelical Christian
Publishers Association

Printed in the United States of America.
5 4 3 2

Contents

Introduction

You stand impatiently backstage, waiting for the announcer to call your name. Sweat beads on your brow, as much from the bright, hot lights as from your nervousness. You're the next contestant on the hit television game show, *A to Z Bible Trivia*!

And now, welcome. . . The voice trails off in your head as you hear your own name spoken. You walk, as if in a dream, past TV cameras and the studio audience. Will your knowledge of the Bible dazzle this crowd enough to turn their polite applause into a hearty ovation?

Now the host of the show speaks:

You know how our game is played—we'll ask you questions from the Bible, and you answer them. Simple enough, right? We shall see. . . .

There are four quizzes for every letter of the alphabet—even for Q and X! Each quiz features five questions, ranging in value from 100 to 500 points—and the questions get harder as the points increase. When you've been through all four quizzes for a particular letter of the alphabet, you'll have the opportunity to Risk It!*—to chance any or all of your points for that letter on one final question. You could potentially double your score!*

7

We'll keep a running tally of your score, and by the end of the show, we'll know whether you belong in the Bible Hall of Fame. . .or the Hall of Shame. Are you ready to begin?

You croak a weak "yes" and make your way to the contestant's chair. Flashing signs prompt the audience to applaud as you await the first question. . . .

Note: The New International Version is the primary translation used in this book. Where wording differs between the NIV and the King James Version, both are listed in the answer section—NIV first, KJV second.

 Are you "able" to handle "Abel"? Most everyone knows Abel was the world's first murder victim. . .but what else do you know about this unfortunate man?

Answers on next page.

100 What "first couple" gave birth to Abel?

200 What unaccepted offering provoked Cain's murder of Abel?

300 What five-word question did Cain use to dismiss God's question about Abel's whereabouts?

400 What part of Abel did God tell Cain "cries out to me from the ground"?

500 What third son did Eve say God gave her in place of the murdered Abel?

Abel answers

100	Adam and Eve (Genesis 4:1–2)
200	fruits of the soil (Genesis 4:3–5)
300	"Am I my brother's keeper?" (Genesis 4:9)
400	his blood (Genesis 4:10)
500	Seth (Genesis 4:25)

Your Score for This Quiz:

_____ Points

You've seen these initials in TV police shows—they stand for "also known as." What do you know about the alternative names of Bible characters?

Answers on next page.

100 What apostle and New Testament author was originally known as Saul?

200 What fisherman turned apostle was also known as Simon or Cephas?

300 What Old Testament prophet once had his name changed to "Belteshazzar"?

400 What nickname, meaning "Son of Encouragement," did the apostles give to Joseph, a Levite from Cyprus?

500 What nickname did Jesus give to the disciple brothers James and John?

AKA answers

100	Paul (Acts 13:9)
200	Peter (John 1:42)
300	Daniel (Daniel 1:7)
400	Barnabas (Acts 4:36)
500	Boanerges, or Sons of Thunder (Mark 3:17)

Your Score for This Quiz:

_____ Points

Cumulative Score, A Quizzes:

_____ Points

A men Brother

When you see a letter or word in quotation marks in the title of a quiz in *A to Z Bible Trivia*, you know that letter or word will appear in the answer to those quiz questions. All of the answers to these questions are men's names starting with *A*.

Answers on next page.

100   What man, brother of Moses, was priest for the nation of Israel?

200   What Caesar ordered the census that brought Mary, expecting the baby Jesus, to Bethlehem?

300   What man, with a name like a Roman god, became a powerful preacher of Christ in the early church?

400   What Old Testament prophet was a shepherd from Tekoa?

500   What cousin of King Saul served as commander of Saul's army?

"A" men, Brother
answers

100	Aaron (Exodus 4:14, 28:1)
200	Augustus (Luke 2:1–5)
300	Apollos (Acts 18:24–26)
400	Amos (Amos 1:1)
500	Abner (1 Samuel 14:51, 17:55)

Your Score for This Quiz:

_____ Points

Cumulative Score, A Quizzes:

_____ Points

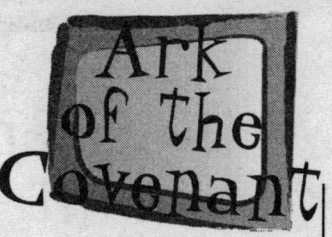

Ark of the Covenant

No, Indiana Jones didn't actually find the ark—that's just Hollywood hype. But the real ark of the covenant was a pretty dramatic thing itself. What do you remember about it?

Answers on next page.

100 What precious metal covered the ark and its carrying poles?

200 What leader, shortly before his death, gave orders to place the Book of the Law beside the ark?

300 Which tribe of Israel had responsibility for moving the ark?

400 What enemies of Israel captured the ark in battle?

500 What river stopped flowing when priests carrying the ark reached the water's edge?

Ark of the Covenant answers

100	gold (Exodus 25:10–14)
200	Moses (Deuteronomy 31:24–26)
300	Levi (Deuteronomy 10:8)
400	the Philistines (1 Samuel 4:10–11)
500	the Jordan (Joshua 3:15–16)

Your Score for This Quiz:

_____ Points

Total Score, A Quizzes:

_____ Points

Risk It!

Anointing

Well, you've completed all four *A* quizzes and reached the *Risk It!* portion of the game. What do you know about biblical anointing? Consider how much of your total score on the *A* quizzes you want to risk on the one question following. If you answer correctly, you add the amount you risked to your total *A* quiz score. . .if you answer incorrectly, you *subtract* the amount you risked. Have you made your decision? Mark down the amount you're willing to risk, and we'll unveil the question. . . .

Your Total Score, A Quizzes:

_____ Points

Your Risk It! Amount:

_____ Points

What prophet anointed the young David as Israel's king to succeed Saul?

Answer on next page.

Risk It! answer

Samuel (1 Samuel 16:12–13)

Your Total Score, A Quizzes:

_____ Points

+ or – Your Risk It! Amount:

_____ Points

Running Total:

_____ Points

Baal's Friends and Foes

Some people loved him, and some people hated him—but he wasn't even real! What do you know about the supporters and opponents of the false god Baal?

Answers on next page.

100 What "fleecy" judge was nicknamed "Jerub-Baal" for tearing down Baal's altar?

200 What prophet of God challenged 450 prophets of Baal to see whose god would answer by fire?

300 What leader's death preceded the Israelites' descent into Baal worship?

400 What evil woman led Israel's King Ahab, her husband, into Baal worship?

500 What king of Israel claimed to worship Baal, only to destroy the priests of Baal?

Baal's Friends and Foes answers

100	Gideon (Judges 6:32)
200	Elijah (1 Kings 18:22–24)
300	Joshua (Judges 2:8–11)
400	Jezebel (1 Kings 16:29–31)
500	Jehu (2 Kings 10:18–19)

Your Score for This Quiz:

_____ Points

Births Foretold

Sure, your mom knew you were coming months before you were born. . .but what about those Bible babies predicted long before they were even *conceived?* Tell us what you remember about these special births.

Answers on next page.

100 What strongman's birth was foretold to his father, Manoah?

200 What angel announced the birth of Jesus to His mother, Mary?

300 What son's birth was foretold to his ninety-nine-year-old father, Abraham?

400 What "wild donkey of a man's" birth was foretold to his mother, Hagar?

500 What boy, destined to become king at age eight, had his birth foretold by a man of God to the wicked King Jeroboam?

Births Foretold answers

100	Samson (Judges 13:2–3, 24)
200	Gabriel (Luke 1:26–31)
300	Isaac (Genesis 18:10–11, 21:1–5)
400	Ishmael (Genesis 16:7–12)
500	Josiah (1 Kings 13:1–2)

Your Score for This Quiz:

_____ Points

Cumulative Score, B Quizzes:

_____ Points

Bread

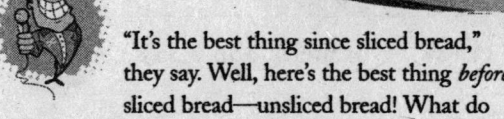

"It's the best thing since sliced bread," they say. Well, here's the best thing *before* sliced bread—unsliced bread! What do you know about bread in the Bible?

Answers on next page.

100 What two words follow Jesus' statement, "I am the bread. . ."?

200 How many loaves of bread, along with two fish, did Jesus turn into a meal for five thousand men?

300 What kind of bread were the Israelites to eat in their Passover celebration?

400 What prophet requested bread from a destitute widow—who then received a miraculous supply of flour and oil?

500 Besides the breaking of bread, what is one of three other things the early church devoted itself to?

Bread answers

100	"of life" (John 6:35)
200	five (Matthew 14:17–21)
300	unleavened (Numbers 9:10–11)
400	Elijah (1 Kings 17:9–16)
500	the apostles' teaching, fellowship, or prayer (Acts 2:42)

Your Score for This Quiz:

_____ Points

Cumulative Score, B Quizzes:

_____ Points

"B"-ware!

Those quotation marks tell you that all of the answers to these questions will start with the letter *B*. Are you ready? "B" alert now. . . .

Answers on next page.

100 Where did God confuse the language of prideful people trying to build a tower to heaven?

200 What product were the Israelites, as slaves of Egypt, forced to make?

300 What greedy prophet was saved from death by a talking donkey?

400 What physical condition of Elisha was once mocked by young people—leading to their mauling by bears?

500 What powerful creature, described in the book of Job, has a tail "like a cedar"?

"B"-ware! answers

100	Babel (Genesis 11:1–9)
200	bricks (Exodus 5:4–8)
300	Balaam (Numbers 22:21–33)
400	baldness (2 Kings 2:23–24)
500	behemoth (Job 40:15–24)

Your Score for This Quiz:

_____ Points

Total Score, B Quizzes:

_____ Points

Risk It!

Barnabas

All right. . .you've navigated the *B* quizzes and it's time for another *Risk It!* question. How much do you know about Barnabas? Consider how much of your total score on the *B* quizzes you want to risk on the one question following. If you answer correctly, you add the amount you risked to your total *B* quiz score. . .if you answer incorrectly, you *subtract* the amount you risked. Ready to decide? Jot down the amount you're willing to risk, and we'll unveil the question. . . .

Your Total Score, B Quizzes:

_____ Points

Your Risk It! Amount:

_____ Points

What cousin of Barnabas, who temporarily deserted the ministry, caused a falling out between Barnabas and the apostle Paul?

Answer on next page.

Risk It! answer

John Mark (Acts 15:37–40)

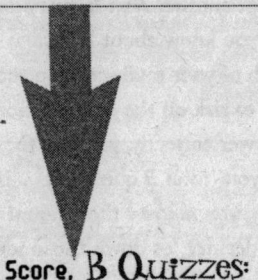

Your Total Score, B Quizzes:

_____ Points

+ or – Your Risk It! Amount:

_____ Points

Running Total (A through B Quizzes):

_____ Points

Ah, the "promised land"—sounds peaceful and serene, doesn't it? Well, not exactly. . .Canaan Land brought its own set of challenges to the Israelites. How much do you remember from your Bible?

Answers on next page.

100   What patriarch was promised the land of Canaan by God?

200   What two foods were said to flow in the land of Canaan?

300   What leader only saw Canaan from a distance, after leading the Israelites on a forty-year journey there?

400   What disaster caused Jacob to send his sons from Canaan to Egypt?

500   What did the fearful Israelite spies who explored Canaan say they looked like compared to the giants they saw there?

Canaan Land
answers

100	Abraham (Genesis 17:3–8)
200	milk and honey (Numbers 13:1, 27)
300	Moses (Deuteronomy 32:48–52)
400	famine (Genesis 42:1–5)
500	grasshoppers (Numbers 13:33)

Your Score for This Quiz:

_____ Points

 Talk about staying power. . .you'll still find the city of Corinth on the map of modern Greece, two thousand years after the apostle Paul wrote letters to a church there! What do you know about their correspondence?

Answers on next page.

100 Which of these three—faith, hope, or love—did Paul say was greatest in a letter to Christians at Corinth?

200 What "prickly" physical ailment did Paul write about to the church at Corinth?

300 What man, along with his wife Priscilla, moved to Corinth from Italy when all Jews were ordered to leave Rome?

400 Who, besides Jews, did Paul preach to every Sabbath day in the Corinth synagogue?

500 What man, for whom a New Testament book is named, traveled to Corinth to help pick up an offering for needy saints?

31

Corinth
answers

100	love (1 Corinthians 13:13)
200	a thorn in the flesh (2 Corinthians 12:7)
300	Aquila (Acts 18:1–2)
400	Greeks (Acts 18:4)
500	Titus (2 Corinthians 8:16–19)

Your Score for This Quiz:

_____ Points

Cumulative Score, C Quizzes:

_____ Points

Creative Answers

Okay, "creative answers" is a nice way of saying "lies." There were some real whoppers told in the Bible! Show us what you know about them.

Answers on next page.

100 What disciple, watching Jesus' arrest and trial, claimed three times that he didn't know the Lord?

200 What relationship did Abram claim to his wife, Sarai, to try to gain favor with the Egyptians?

300 What did the murderous King Herod tell the wise men he wanted to do to the young boy Jesus?

400 What husband and wife died after lying about the amount of money they gave as an offering?

500 What explanation did Jewish priests and Roman soldiers give for the disappearance of Jesus' body after the Resurrection?

Creative Answers
answers

100	Peter (Matthew 26:69–75)
200	brother to sister (Genesis 12:10–20)
300	worship Him (Matthew 2:7–8)
400	Ananias and Sapphira (Acts 5:1–11)
500	that it was stolen by the disciples (Matthew 28:11–15)

Your Score for This Quiz:

_____ Points

Cumulative Score, C Quizzes:

_____ Points

The *C* in this quiz title is in quotation marks—and that's your hint that all of the answers begin with the third letter of the alphabet. Let's "c" how you do with these questions!

Answers on next page.

100 What did Jesus say was more likely to go through the eye of a needle than for a rich man to enter heaven?

200 What occupation did Joseph, Jesus' earthly father, practice?

300 What moldable material, according to Jeremiah, represented Israel in the hands of God?

400 What color did Isaiah use to describe sin?

500 What vegetable did the complaining Israelites recall from their years of slavery in Egypt?

"C" Ya answers

100	camel (Matthew 19:24)
200	carpentry (Matthew 13:53–55)
300	clay (Jeremiah 18:1–6)
400	crimson (Isaiah 1:18)
500	cucumbers (Numbers 11:4–5)

Your Score for This Quiz:

_____ Points

Total Score, C Quizzes:

_____ Points

Risk It!

Commandments

Congratulations—you've reached the *Risk It!* section for the *C* quizzes. Feel confident on the Ten Commandments? Decide how much of your total score on the *C* quizzes you want to risk on the one question following. If you answer correctly, you add the amount you risked to your total *C* quiz score. . .if you answer incorrectly, you *subtract* the amount you risked. Made your decision? Write down the amount you're willing to risk, and we'll unveil the question. . . .

Your Total Score, C Quizzes:

_____ Points

Your Risk It! Amount:

_____ Points

What issue does the last of the Ten Commandments address?

Answer on next page.

Risk It! answer

coveting (Exodus 20:17)

Your Total Score, C Quizzes:

_____ **Points**

+ or – Your Risk It! Amount:

_____ **Points**

Running Total (A through C Quizzes):

_____ **Points**

Daniel's story

Any kid in Sunday school can give you the highlights of Daniel's story. What do *you* know about him?

Answers on next page.

100 What illegal activity resulted in Daniel being thrown into the lions' den?

200 What are the better-known names of Daniel's friends Hananiah, Mishael, and Azariah?

300 What miraculous sign, interpreted by Daniel, foretold the doom of King Belshazzar?

400 What was the composition of the feet of an enormous statue in King Nebuchadnezzar's dream—explained by Daniel?

500 What angel appears twice in the story of Daniel to explain the prophet's visions?

Daniel's Story answers

100	praying to God (Daniel 6:6–14)
200	Shadrach, Meshach, and Abednego (Daniel 1:7)
300	the handwriting on the wall (Daniel 5:1–31)
400	iron and clay (Daniel 2:32–33)
500	Gabriel (Daniel 8:15–16, 9:21)

Your Score for This Quiz:

_____ **Points**

Demons, Begone

They call it an "exorcism"—making a demon (or demons) leave a possessed person. Kind of creepy, huh? It happened a lot in Bible times—how many do you recall?

Answers on next page.

100 What kind of animals rushed into a lake and drowned after receiving demons cast from humans?

200 What name did a wild man, possessed by many demons, give in answer to Jesus' question?

300 How many demons were cast out of Mary Magdalene?

400 What "skill" did a young slave girl lose when Paul cast a demon from her?

500 What specific activity did Jesus sometimes forbid to newly cast-out demons?

Demons, Begone answers

100	pigs (Matthew 8:28–32)
200	Legion (Mark 5:6–9)
300	seven (Luke 8:2)
400	fortune-telling (Acts 16:16–19)
500	speaking (Mark 1:34, Luke 4:40–41)

Your Score for This Quiz:

_____ Points

Cumulative Score, D Quizzes:

_____ Points

Disasters

Long before the *Titanic* tragedy or the San Francisco earthquake, there were major disasters in the Bible. Tell us what you know about these five.

Answers on next page.

100 What widespread lack of food forced the patriarch Isaac to leave his home and move to another country?

200 What swarming insects stripped Egypt of every green plant in the eighth plague called down by Moses?

300 What transportation disaster befell the apostle Paul as he was traveling to Rome to stand trial before Caesar?

400 What fraction of Earth's population is killed by the horses and riders of the Revelation's sixth trumpet judgment?

500 What collapsed and killed eighteen people in a "news event" that Jesus used to encourage repentance?

Disasters answers

100	famine (Genesis 26:1)
200	locusts (Exodus 10:13–15)
300	shipwreck (Acts 27:21–44)
400	one-third (Revelation 9:13–19)
500	a tower (Luke 13:2–5)

Your Score for This Quiz:

_____ Points

Cumulative Score, D Quizzes:

_____ Points

"D"-Tails

There's a set of quotation marks around that *D*, so you already have a clue as to how the answers to these five questions begin.

Answers on next page.

100   What kind of bird, released from the ark, brought an olive leaf back to Noah?

200   What substance did God use to form the first man?

300   What prophetess, the wife of Lappidoth, was a judge of Israel?

400   What did scoffers accuse the disciples of when they spoke in tongues at Pentecost?

500   What Philistine idol fell over and broke in pieces when the ark of the covenant was placed nearby?

"D"-tails answers

100	dove (Genesis 8:11)
200	dust (Genesis 2:7)
300	Deborah (Judges 4:4)
400	drunkenness (Acts 2:1–15)
500	Dagon (1 Samuel 5:1–5)

Your Score for This Quiz:

_____ Points

Total Score, D Quizzes:

_____ Points

Risk It!

Donkeys

The *D* questions are history. . . . Now it's time to *Risk It!* What do you remember about donkeys of the Bible? Choose how much of your total score on the *D* quizzes you want to risk on the one question following. If you answer correctly, you add the amount you risked to your total *D* quiz score. . .if you answer incorrectly, you *subtract* the amount you risked. Made up your mind yet? Note the amount you're willing to risk, and we'll unveil the question. . . .

Your Total Score, D Quizzes:

_____ Points

Your Risk It! Amount:

_____ Points

What part of a dead donkey did Samson use to kill one thousand enemy Philistines?

Answer on next page.

Risk It! answer

a jawbone (Judges 15:14–16)

Your Total Score, D Quizzes:

_____ Points

+ or – Your Risk It! Amount:

_____ Points

Running Total (A through D Quizzes):

_____ Points

Earthquake!

 Talk about shaking things up. . .earthquakes are a relatively common occurrence in the pages of the Bible. How's your seismological knowledge?

Answers on next page.

100   What kind of creature started an earthquake by rolling back the stone that sealed Jesus' tomb?

200   What mountain, where Moses received the Ten Commandments, shook as the Lord came down on it?

300   What missionary companion of Paul experienced an earthquake in a Philippian jail?

400   What prophet went through an earthquake only to learn that God spoke in a gentle whisper?

500   What is one of three miracles accompanying the earthquake that occurred at the moment of Jesus' death?

Earthquake!
answers

100   an angel (Matthew 28:1–4)

200   Mount Sinai (Exodus 19:18–19)

300   Silas (Acts 16:25–28)

400   Elijah (1 Kings 19:11–13)

500   temple curtain torn from top to
       bottom; tombs broke open; bodies
       of dead saints raised to life
       (Matthew 27:50–53)

Your Score for This Quiz:

_____ Points

Engaging Stories

Yes, this quiz title has a double meaning—the stories are "engaging" in that they catch your interest. . .but they're also all about people getting married. What do you know about these Bible couples?

Answers on next page.

100 What man was planning to wed Mary when she was found to be pregnant through the Holy Spirit?

200 What woman lay at the feet of Boaz in a threshing floor—initiating a relationship that culminated in marriage?

300 What woman was Jacob tricked into marrying by his devious uncle Laban?

400 What nationality of woman did Samson, to his parents' disgust, seek out for a wife?

500 What daughter did Reuel, a priest of Midian, give to Moses as his wife?

Engaging
Stories answers

100	Joseph (Matthew 1:18)
200	Ruth (Ruth 3:7–8, 4:13)
300	Leah (Genesis 29:21–23)
400	Philistine (Judges 14:1–3)
500	Zipporah (Exodus 2:16–21)

Your Score for This Quiz:

_____ Points

Cumulative Score, E Quizzes:

_____ Points

"E"-vents

And now the quotation marks surround the fifth letter of the alphabet—with every answer in this quiz starting with *E*. Excellent!

Answers on next page.

100 Where did God plant a garden and place the man, Adam, He had created?

200 What nationality was the man a young Moses killed and hid in the sand?

300 What kind of man did the apostle Philip find in a chariot, reading from the book of Isaiah?

400 What kind of lamb did the prophet Nathan mention in a story that exposed sin in King David's life?

500 What priestly garment did David use to ask God whether he should pursue the Amalekites, who had kidnapped two of his wives?

"E"-vents answers

100	Eden (Genesis 2:8)
200	Egyptian (Exodus 2:11–12)
300	Ethiopian eunuch (either answer acceptable) (Acts 8:26–35)
400	ewe (2 Samuel 12:1–6)
500	ephod (1 Samuel 30:1–8)

Your Score for This Quiz:

_____ Points

Cumulative Score, E Quizzes:

_____ Points

Ezekiel's Visions

If you eat pizza right before bedtime, you might have some strange dreams. . .but probably nothing like the visions the prophet Ezekiel had! What do you recall of them?

Answers on next page.

100 What round objects did Ezekiel see accompanying four unusual "living creatures"?

200 What gruesome things did Ezekiel see filling a valley?

300 What heavenly body did Ezekiel see some two dozen men bowing to at the entrance to God's temple?

400 What unusual "meal" did Ezekiel eat in the vision that brought him God's calling?

500 What kind of tool did Ezekiel see a bronzed man using on a new temple on a high mountain?

Ezekiel's Visions answers

100	wheels (Ezekiel 1:15–21)
200	dry bones (Ezekiel 37:1–14)
300	the sun (Ezekiel 8:16)
400	a scroll, or the "roll of a book" (Ezekiel 2:9–3:2)
500	a measuring rod, or reed (Ezekiel 40:1–3)

Your Score for This Quiz:

_____ Points

Total Score, E Quizzes:

_____ Points

Risk It!

Extra-Long Words

And now you can *Risk It!* for the four *E* quizzes as we test your knowledge of extra-long words. Consider how much of your total score on the *E* quizzes you want to risk on the one question to follow. If you answer correctly, you add the amount you risked to your total *E* quiz score. . .if you answer incorrectly, you *subtract* the amount you risked. Settled on a number? Write down the amount you're willing to risk, and we'll unveil the question. . . .

Your Total Score, E Quizzes:

_____ Points

Your Risk It! Amount:

_____ Points

What fourteen-letter word defined the ministry that Paul told the Corinthians God has given those who are in Christ?

Answer on next page.

Risk It! answer

reconciliation (2 Corinthians 5:18)

Your Total Score, E Quizzes:

_____ Points

+ or – Your Risk It! Amount:

_____ Points

Running Total (A through E Quizzes):

_____ Points

Fathers

They say George Washington was the "father of his country"—but who was the father of George? Here are some questions about *biblical* fathers—we'll name the kids, you name the dad.

Answers on next page.

100 Who was the father of Solomon?

200 Who was the father of Benjamin?

300 Who was the father of James and John?

400 Who was the father of Joshua?

500 Who was the father of Gershom?

Fathers answers

100	David (2 Samuel 12:24)
200	Jacob, or Israel (Genesis 46:19)
300	Zebedee (Mark 1:19–20)
400	Nun (Numbers 11:28)
500	Moses (Exodus 2:21–22)

Your Score for This Quiz:

_____ Points

 "Filthy animal" isn't just an insult—it was a reality for the biblical Israelites. God called many animals "unclean," and they were not to be touched or eaten. Tell us what you know about them.

Answers on next page.

100 What kind of animal was the "prodigal son" feeding when he realized he should return home to his father?

200 What color-changing lizard was not permitted on Israelite menus?

300 What soaring bird, mentioned in Isaiah 40, led Moses' list of flying creatures that could not be eaten?

400 What bird, which brought food to Elijah, was deemed unclean in the laws of God?

500 What beast of burden was forbidden as food to the Israelites?

61

Filthy
Animals answers

100	pigs (Luke 15:11–20)
200	chameleon (Leviticus 11:29–30)
300	eagle (Leviticus 11:13–19)
400	raven (1 Kings 17:1–4, Deuteronomy 14:11–14)
500	camel (Leviticus 11:4)

Your Score for This Quiz:

_____ Points

Cumulative Score, F Quizzes:

_____ Points

Food

They didn't have McDonald's back then, but the people of the Bible loved to eat just like we do. What do you know about biblical foods?

Answers on next page.

100 What did Samson eat from the carcass of a lion he had killed?

200 What insect made a large part of the diet of John the Baptist?

300 What did Jesus eat in the presence of His disciples shortly after His resurrection?

400 What is one of the two kinds of cakes Abigail brought to King David to apologize for her husband's rude behavior?

500 What kind of plants and trees did God tell Adam and Eve they could use for food?

Food answers

100	honey (Judges 14:5–9)
200	locusts (Matthew 3:4)
300	broiled fish (Luke 24:36–43)
400	raisin or fig (1 Samuel 25:18–25)
500	seed bearing (Genesis 1:27–29)

Your Score for This Quiz:

_____ Points

Cumulative Score, F Quizzes:

_____ Points

Future Things

You can't say what's going to happen to you tomorrow. . .but God knows the future as if it's the present. Show us your knowledge of the future things found in the Bible.

Answers on next page.

100 What did Jesus say He would arrive in when He returns to earth "with power and great glory"?

200 What special headwear will be the heavenly reward for faithful service on earth?

300 What two animals represent the saved and lost people of earth, whom Jesus will separate at the final judgment?

400 What "lake" is the final, eternal home for those people whose names are not found in the book of life?

500 How many years, according to John's Revelation, will Jesus reign on earth before Satan's final judgment?

Future Things answers

100	a cloud (Luke 21:27)
200	a crown (2 Timothy 4:8, James 1:12)
300	sheep and goats (Matthew 25:31–33)
400	the lake of fire (Revelation 20:15)
500	one thousand (Revelation 20:6–10)

Your Score for This Quiz:

_____ Points

Total Score, F Quizzes:

_____ Points

Risk It!

Famous Fruit

Well, you've gotten through all four *F* quizzes and reached the *Risk It!* portion of the game. Let's test your knowledge of the "famous fruit" of the Bible. Think over how much of your total score on the *F* quizzes you want to risk on the one question following. If you answer correctly, you add the amount you risked to your total *F* quiz score. . .if you answer incorrectly, you *subtract* the amount you risked. Have you decided? Mark down the amount you're willing to risk, and we'll unveil the question. . . .

Your Total Score, *F* Quizzes:

_____ Points

Your Risk It! Amount:

_____ Points

What is the last of the ninefold "fruit of the spirit" mentioned in Galatians 5?

Answer on next page.

Risk It! answer

self-control, or temperance (Galatians 5:22–23)

Your Total Score, F Quizzes:

_____ Points

+ or – Your Risk It! Amount:

_____ Points

Running Total (A through F Quizzes):

_____ Points

Golgotha

You may already know that Golgotha is the place where Jesus was crucified. But what else do you know about this somber locale?

Answers on next page.

100 How many criminals were crucified with Jesus at Golgotha?

200 What part of the body completes the meaning of the name Golgotha: "The place of the. . ."?

300 How did the soldiers at Golgotha decide who should receive Jesus' clothing?

400 What did mocking soldiers offer Jesus to drink while He hung on the cross at Golgotha?

500 How many languages appeared on the sign—reading "The King of the Jews"—that hung on Jesus' cross?

Golgotha answers

100	two (Mark 15:27)
200	skull (John 19:17)
300	by casting lots (John 19:23–24)
400	vinegar, or wine mixed with myrrh (Luke 23:36, Mark 15:23)
500	three (John 19:19–20)

Your Score for This Quiz:

_____ Points

It's a common theme in the Bible—paying back good for evil done. Here are five examples. . .what do you remember about them?

Answers on next page.

100 What did Jesus command His followers to show to their enemies?

200 What Israelite, as a powerful official in Egypt, forgave his brothers who years before had sold him into slavery?

300 What did Jesus tell His disciples to do to the people who cursed them?

400 Who did Moses ask God to heal—after God struck her with leprosy for murmuring against Moses' foreign wife?

500 What servant of the high priest had his ear sliced off by Peter's sword—then restored by Jesus—during Jesus' arrest?

Good for Evil answers

100	love (Luke 6:35)
200	Joseph (Genesis 50:15–21)
300	bless them (Luke 6:28)
400	Miriam (Numbers 12:1–13)
500	Malchus (Luke 22:50–51, John 18:10)

Your Score for This Quiz:

_____ Points

Cumulative Score, G Quizzes:

_____ Points

 You guessed it—all of the answers in this quiz are places that start with *G*. Go for it!

Answers on next page.

100 What wicked city did Jesus pair with Sodom?

200 What sea was the location of Jesus' calling of Peter and Andrew?

300 Where did Jesus pray—and His disciples sleep—the night He was betrayed and arrested?

400 What mount saw the deaths of King Saul and his sons in battle?

500 What city's name appears in the name of its "biggest" resident—Goliath?

"G" o To answers

100	Gomorrah (Matthew 10:15)
200	Galilee (Matthew 4:18–19)
300	Gethsemane (Matthew 26:36–46)
400	Gilboa (1 Samuel 31:8)
500	Gath (1 Samuel 17:4)

Your Score for This Quiz:

_____ Points

Cumulative Score, G Quizzes:

_____ Points

Guilty!

At fault, caught, busted. . .any way you look at it, *guilty*. What do you know about these five "cases" from the Bible?

Answers on next page.

100 Who did Adam blame when God confronted him about eating the forbidden fruit?

200 What sin was a woman caught in by scribes and Pharisees who then tried to trick Jesus into approving her death by stoning?

300 What sin against the Holy Spirit, according to Jesus, would result in eternal guilt?

400 Who was stoned to death after admitting he had stolen clothing, silver, and gold from the ruins of Jericho?

500 What priests, the two sons of Eli, were judged for treating the Lord's offerings with contempt?

Guilty! answers

100	the woman, Eve (Genesis 3:11–12)
200	adultery (John 8:1–11)
300	blasphemy (Mark 3:28–29)
400	Achan (Joshua 7:19–25)
500	Hophni and Phinehas (1 Samuel 1:3, 2:12–17)

Your Score for This Quiz:

_____ Points

Total Score, G Quizzes:

_____ Points

Risk It!

Gideon

It's time to *Risk It!* for the *G* quizzes. What do you know about Gideon? Think about how much of your total score on the *G* quizzes you want to risk on the one question following. If you answer correctly, you add the amount you risked to your total *G* quiz score. . .if you answer incorrectly, you *subtract* the amount you risked. Got your number? Mark down the amount you're willing to risk, and we'll unveil the question. . . .

Your Total Score, G Quizzes:

_____ Points

Your Risk It! Amount:

_____ Points

What substance appeared on Gideon's fleece one night—but not the next—to convince him he was working in God's will?

Answer on next page.

Risk It! answer

dew (Judges 6:36–40)

Your Total Score, G Quizzes:

_____ Points

+ or – Your Risk It! Amount:

_____ Points

Running Total (A through G Quizzes):

_____ Points

Hairy People

There are plenty of things a person can be known for. Here are five Bible characters who were famous for their hair. Are you "brushed up" on this category?

Answers on next page.

100 What Bible strongman lost his power when his long hair was cut off?

200 What twin brother of Jacob was born hairy?

300 What son of David cut his long hair whenever it became too heavy for him?

400 What did the apostle Paul say that long hair is to a woman?

500 What does the "lover" in the Song of Songs twice compare his "beloved's" hair to?

Hairy
People answers

100	Samson (Judges 16:15–20)
200	Esau (Genesis 25:25–26)
300	Absalom (2 Samuel 14:25–26)
400	glory (1 Corinthians 11:15)
500	a flock of goats (Song of Songs 4:1, 6:5)

Your Score for This Quiz:

_____ Points

Heavenly Sounds

Now hear this. . . . The Bible tells of many different sounds from heaven. What do you know about the five following?

Answers on next page.

100 What event in Jesus' life featured a voice from heaven saying, "This is my Son, whom I love"?

200 What sound from heaven accompanied God's work at Pentecost?

300 What musical instrument accompanies the song of victorious saints in heaven, according to John's Revelation?

400 What sound, according to the apostle Paul, causes every knee in heaven to bow?

500 What does the voice of the "living creature" resemble when the Lamb breaks the first seal on the seven-sealed book of Revelation?

Heavenly Sounds answers

100	His baptism (Matthew 3:16–17)
200	a violent, or mighty, wind (Acts 2:1–4)
300	harps (Revelation 15:1–4)
400	the name of Jesus (Philippians 2:10)
500	thunder (Revelation 5:1, 6:1)

Your Score for This Quiz:

_____ Points

Cumulative Score, H Quizzes:

_____ Points

The *H* in quotation marks means every answer will start with that letter. And here's another hint: Each answer is a person's name. . . .

Answers on next page.

100 What woman, the wife of Elkanah, was mother of the prophet Samuel?

200 What Old Testament prophet, at God's command, married an adulterous woman named Gomer?

300 What wicked New Testament king "was eaten by worms and died" for allowing people to call him a god?

400 What king of Tyre supplied cedar logs to Solomon for building the Lord's temple?

500 What prophetess told the faithful King Josiah he would not see the disaster God was bringing on his unfaithful nation?

"H"ello There answers

100	Hannah (1 Samuel 1:19–20)
200	Hosea (Hosea 1:2–3)
300	Herod (Acts 12:21–23)
400	Hiram (1 Kings 5:1–12)
500	Huldah (2 Kings 22:14–20)

Your Score for This Quiz:

_____ Points

Cumulative Score, H Quizzes:

_____ Points

You'll note that the word *holy* is in quotation marks—so every answer will be a phrase featuring that word.

Answers on next page.

100 What did Jesus promise that God the Father would give to anyone who asked?

200 What did God tell Moses he was standing on when he approached the burning bush?

300 What did John call the new Jerusalem he saw in a vision, coming down out of heaven?

400 What did Paul tell Timothy that Christians should lift up in prayer?

500 What four-word phrase is used often in the book of Isaiah to describe the Lord?

"Holy," Holy, Holy answers

100	the Holy Spirit (Luke 11:11–13)
200	holy ground (Exodus 3:3–5)
300	the Holy City (Revelation 21:1–2)
400	holy hands (1 Timothy 2:8)
500	"Holy One of Israel" (see, for example, Isaiah 49:7)

Your Score for This Quiz:

_____ Points

Total Score, H Quizzes:

_____ Points

Risk It!

Hard Labor

All right. . .you've completed the *H* quizzes, and it's time to *Risk It!* How confident are you on the category "Hard Labor"? Consider how much of your total score on the *H* quizzes you want to risk on the one question following. If you answer correctly, you add the amount you risked to your total *H* quiz score. . .if you answer incorrectly, you *subtract* the amount you risked. Are you ready? Write down the amount you're willing to risk, and we'll unveil the question. . . .

Your Total Score, H Quizzes:

_____ Points

Your Risk It! Amount:

_____ Points

What body fluid was part of the curse that came by Adam and Eve's sin?

Answer on next page.

87

Risk It! answer

sweat (Genesis 3:19)

Your Total Score, H Quizzes:

_____ Points

+ or – Your Risk It! Amount:

_____ Points

Running Total (A through H Quizzes):

_____ Points

We certainly hope you know these answers, which all begin with the letter *I*. Go ahead—impress us with your intellect!

Answers on next page.

100 What lodging place in Bethlehem turned away Joseph and his very expectant wife, Mary?

200 What metal, used to sharpen other like metal, does Proverbs compare to friends?

300 What kind of place was Patmos, where John received his Revelation of Jesus Christ?

400 What major prophet had a son named Shear-Jashub?

500 What does the apostle Paul urge Christians to be "...of God"?

"I" Know answers

100	inn (Luke 2:4–7)
200	iron (Proverbs 27:17)
300	island (Revelation 1:9)
400	Isaiah (Isaiah 7:3)
500	imitators (Ephesians 5:1)

Your Score for This Quiz:

_____ Points

Imprisoned

Long before Monopoly popularized the "Get Out of Jail Free" card, these Bible characters found themselves stuck in a jail cell without one! What do you know about their stories?

Answers on next page.

100 What handsome son of Jacob was imprisoned after a false report from Potiphar's wife?

200 What wandering preacher was imprisoned for challenging the adulterous marriage of King Herod?

300 What notorious prisoner gained his freedom from Pontius Pilate as Jesus was sentenced to crucifixion?

400 What "weeping prophet" was imprisoned in a dungeon on false charges of deserting to the enemy?

500 What two things were Paul and Silas doing at midnight while imprisoned in a Philippian jail?

Imprisoned
answers

100	Joseph (Genesis 39:2–20)
200	John the Baptist (Mark 6:14–18)
300	Barabbas (Matthew 27:24–26)
400	Jeremiah (Jeremiah 37:12–16)
500	praying and singing to God (Acts 16:22–25)

Your Score for This Quiz:

_____ Points

Cumulative Score, I Quizzes:

_____ Points

Insects

Don't let this category bug you. . . . All you need to do is answer five questions involving insects in the Bible.

Answers on next page.

100 What hardworking insect does the book of Proverbs tell lazy people to learn from?

200 What insects are mentioned by the writer of the book of James as destroyers of clothing?

300 What insect swarmed Egypt in the fourth plague on Pharaoh—but stayed out of the land of Goshen where God's people lived?

400 What tiny insect did Jesus say the hypocritical Pharisees strained out of their food, only to "swallow a camel"?

500 What stinging insect did God use to drive enemy peoples out of the Promised Land?

Insects answers

100	ants (Proverbs 6:6–8)
200	moths (James 5:2)
300	flies (Exodus 8:20–24)
400	gnat (Matthew 23:23–24)
500	hornet (Joshua 24:11–12)

Your Score for This Quiz:

_____ Points

Cumulative Score, I Quizzes:

_____ Points

We're not talking about the hymn writer, Watts; the scientist, Newton; or the science-fiction wiz, Asimov. . . . The Isaac in this category is a biblical patriarch. How well do you know his story?

Answers on next page.

100 What "father of many nations" was first of all father to Isaac?

200 What did Isaac's elderly mother, Sarah, do when she was told she would give birth to Isaac?

300 What was the name of Isaac's older half-brother?

400 Where did God tell Isaac's father to sacrifice the young man as a burnt offering?

500 What did the Philistines, envious of Isaac's wealth in flocks and herds, try to destroy?

Isaac answers

100	Abraham (Genesis 17:5, 21:3)
200	laugh (Genesis 18:10–12)
300	Ishmael (Genesis 25:12)
400	Moriah (Genesis 22:1–2)
500	wells (Genesis 26:12–15)

Your Score for This Quiz:

_____ Points

Total Score, I Quizzes:

_____ Points

Risk It!

Initials

Here we are at the *Risk It!* category for the four *I* quizzes. Let's test your knowledge of initials of the Bible. Decide how much of your total score on the *I* quizzes you want to risk on the one question following. If you answer correctly, you add the amount you risked to your total *I* quiz score. . .if you answer incorrectly, you *subtract* the amount you risked. Have a figure in mind? Mark down the amount you're willing to risk, and we'll unveil the question. . . .

Your Total Score, I Quizzes:

_____ Points

Your Risk It! Amount:

_____ Points

Who is J. of A.—a secret disciple who cared for Jesus' body after the crucifixion?

Answer on next page.

Risk It! answer

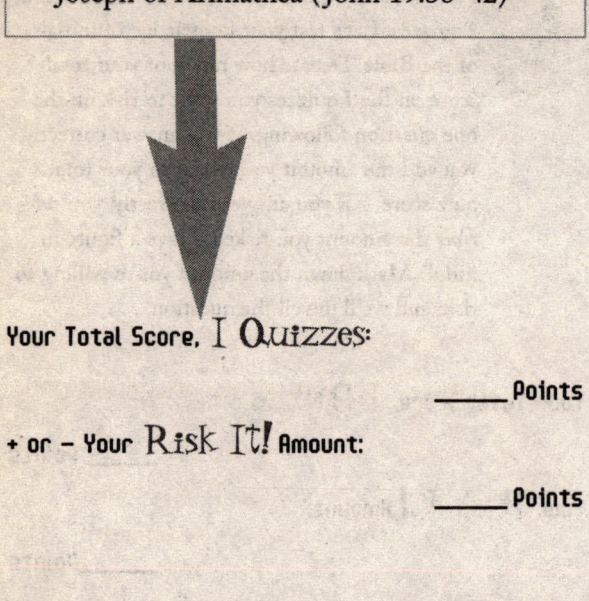

Joseph of Arimathea (John 19:38–42)

Your Total Score, I Quizzes:

_____ **Points**

+ or – Your Risk It! Amount:

_____ **Points**

Running Total (A through I Quizzes):

_____ **Points**

Way back in Bible times, a man named Jesse had several sons. Tell us what you know about Jesse's boys.

Answers on next page.

100 What youngest boy of Jesse was anointed by the prophet Samuel to be king?

200 What town, where years later Jesus would be born, was home to Jesse's boys?

300 What enemies were Jesse's oldest boys, as members of the Israelite army, opposing in the Valley of Elah?

400 How many boys in all did Jesse have?

500 Who was Jesse's firstborn boy?

Jesse's Boys answers

100	David (1 Samuel 16:13)
200	Bethlehem (1 Samuel 17:58)
300	Philistines (1 Samuel 17:17–19)
400	eight (1 Samuel 16:10–11)
500	Eliab (1 Samuel 17:28)

Your Score for This Quiz:

_____ Points

 They say that diamonds are a girl's best friend. . .but God must like jewels, too. What do you recall of the precious stones scattered through the pages of the Bible?

Answers on next page.

100 What valuable red stones, according to Proverbs, are worth less than either wisdom or a good wife?

200 What green stone resembles the rainbow circling God's throne in heaven?

300 How many precious stones, representing the tribes of Israel, were part of the breastplate worn by Old Testament priests?

400 What jewel did Jesus warn against throwing to pigs?

500 What part of the city wall of the New Jerusalem is decorated with precious stones?

Jewels answers

100	rubies (Proverbs 8:11, 31:10)
200	emerald (Revelation 4:1–3)
300	twelve (Exodus 28:15–21)
400	pearls (Matthew 7:6)
500	the foundations (Revelation 21:1–21)

Your Score for This Quiz:

_____ Points

Cumulative Score, J Quizzes:

_____ Points

You probably know something about the suffering saint named Job. . .but do you know enough to complete this quiz? Let's find out!

Answers on next page.

100 What accuser received God's permission to attack Job's possessions, family, and health?

200 What four words of (bad) advice did Job's wife have for her husband?

300 How did Job, defending God's right to give and take away, describe himself upon entering and departing this world?

400 What was the two-letter name of Job's homeland?

500 What trio of friends offered Job plenty of advice but little comfort throughout his trials?

Job answers

100	Satan (Job 1:12, 2:6–7)
200	"Curse God and die" (Job 2:9)
300	naked (Job 1:20–22)
400	Uz (Job 1:1)
500	Eliphaz, Bildad, and Zophar (Job 2:11 and following)

Your Score for This Quiz:

_____ Points

Cumulative Score, J Quizzes:

_____ Points

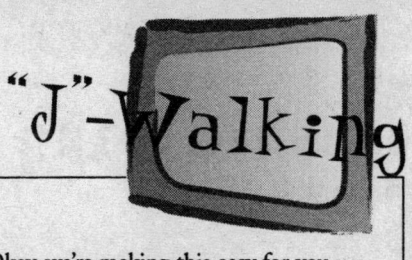

"J"-Walking

Okay, we're making this easy for you. The quotation marks give you an automatic hint to the answers to these questions: They'll all start with the letter *J*.

Answers on next page.

100 What was the first name of the traitorous disciple Iscariot?

200 What son of Saul loved his friend David "as himself"?

300 What synagogue official saw his twelve-year-old daughter raised to life by Jesus?

400 What priest of Midian was father-in-law to Moses?

500 What woman helped Deborah earn a complete military victory by driving a tent peg through the head of the sleeping enemy commander, Sisera?

"J"-Walking
answers

100	Judas (Luke 6:16)
200	Jonathan (1 Samuel 18:1)
300	Jairus (Luke 8:41–56)
400	Jethro (Exodus 3:1)
500	Jael (Judges 4:17–21)

Your Score for This Quiz:

_____ Points

Total Score, J Quizzes:

_____ Points

Risk It!

Judge and Jury

You've gotten through the *J* quizzes. . .and now you'll *Risk It!* How does this "Judge and Jury" category sound to you? Think over how much of your total score on the *J* quizzes you want to risk on the one question following. If you answer correctly, you add the amount you risked to your total *J* quiz score. . .if you answer incorrectly, you *subtract* the amount you risked. Have a figure in mind? Mark down the amount you're willing to risk, and we'll unveil the question. . . .

Your Total Score, *J* Quizzes:

_____ Points

Your Risk It! Amount:

_____ Points

What two words describe the throne on which God sits while passing final judgment on those who have died?

Answer on next page.

Risk It! answer

"great white" (Revelation 20:11)

Your Total Score, J Quizzes:

_____ Points

+ or – Your Risk It! Amount:

_____ Points

Running Total (A through J Quizzes):

_____ Points

Kingdom of Heaven

Jesus had a lot to say about the kingdom of heaven—what it's like, where you find it, who's a part of it. How well do you remember His words?

Answers on next page.

100 What tiny seed did Jesus liken the kingdom of heaven to?

200 What door-openers to the kingdom of heaven did Jesus say He would give to Peter?

300 What group of people, whom the disciples tried to keep from Jesus, did Jesus say are true possessors of the kingdom of heaven?

400 What repetitive phrase, according to Jesus, will not guarantee entry into the kingdom of heaven?

500 What two groups, according to Jesus in the Beatitudes, would inherit the kingdom of heaven?

Kingdom of Heaven answers

100	mustard (Matthew 13:31–32)
200	keys (Matthew 16:15–19)
300	little children (Matthew 19:14)
400	"Lord, Lord" (Matthew 7:21)
500	the poor in spirit, those persecuted for righteousness (Matthew 5:3, 10)

Your Score for This Quiz:

_____ Points

Kings of Earth

We're not talking Burger King, here. . .
we want to know what you know about
the men who ruled the nations of
Bible times.

Answers on next page.

100 Which apostle defended himself before a king named Agrippa—and tried to convert him in the process?

200 What king unwittingly signed a decree that caused his friend, Daniel, to be thrown into a den of lions?

300 What prophet had a dramatic vision and calling from God in the year that King Uzziah died?

400 What king of Persia permitted the Jews in his realm to return to Jerusalem to rebuild the temple?

500 What king of Gath fell for David's trick of feigning insanity—and let him go free?

Kings of Earth answers

100	Paul (Acts 25:13–26:28)
200	Darius (Daniel 6:1–16)
300	Isaiah (Isaiah 6:1–8)
400	Cyrus (Ezra 1:1–4)
500	Achish (1 Samuel 21:10–15)

Your Score for This Quiz:

_____ Points

Cumulative Score, K Quizzes:

_____ Points

Kiss Me

They weren't always romantic, but there are several stories of kisses in the Bible. What do you recall about the following?

Answers on next page.

100 What disciple betrayed Jesus with a kiss?

200 What best friend of David kissed him when David fled from King Saul?

300 What part of Jesus' body did a sinful woman anoint with perfume and kiss during a dinner at a Pharisee's house?

400 What future wife did Jacob kiss the first time he met her—as she watered a flock of sheep?

500 What kind of kiss did the apostle Paul tell the Corinthians to greet each other with?

Kiss Me answers

100   Judas Iscariot (Mark 14:43–45, John 6:70–71)

200   Jonathan (1 Samuel 20:41–42)

300   His feet (Luke 7:36–38)

400   Rachel (Genesis 29:9–11)

500   holy (1 Corinthians 16:20, 2 Corinthians 13:12)

Your Score for This Quiz:

_____ Points

Cumulative Score, K Quizzes:

_____ Points

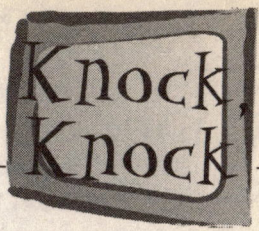

Knock, Knock

No, it's not the opening of a silly joke. In this category, you'll need to show your knowledge of "knocking" in the Bible.

Answers on next page.

100 What two commands on prayer, besides "knock," did Jesus give during His Sermon on the Mount?

200 What servant girl, in her excitement at learning Peter was out of prison and at the door, left him knocking while she ran to tell the other disciples?

300 What did Jesus say servants should be doing when their master, returning from a wedding banquet, knocked on the door?

400 What did Jesus tell church members in Laodicea He would do with them if they opened the door to His knocking?

500 What kind of knocking accompanied the handwriting on the wall that terrified the Babylonian king Belshazzar?

Knock, Knock answers

100	ask and seek (Matthew 7:7–8)
200	Rhoda (Acts 12:12–16)
300	watching (Luke 12:35–38)
400	eat with them (Revelation 3:20)
500	the knocking together of the king's knees (Daniel 5:1–6)

Your Score for This Quiz:

_____ Points

Total Score, K Quizzes:

_____ Points

Risk It!

Kneeling

It's time again to *Risk It!*—this time, for your score on the four *K* quizzes. We're talking about kneeling in the Bible. Decide how much of your total score on the *K* quizzes you want to risk on the one question following. If you answer correctly, you add the amount you risked to your total *K* quiz score. . .if you answer incorrectly, you *subtract* the amount you risked. Are you ready? Jot down the amount you're willing to risk, and we'll unveil the question. . . .

Your Total Score, K Quizzes:

_____ Points

Your Risk It! Amount:

_____ Points

What woman, also known as Tabitha, was raised from the dead after Peter knelt and prayed?

Answer on next page.

Risk It! answer

Dorcas (Acts 9:36–41)

Your Total Score, K Quizzes:

_____ Points

+ or – Your Risk It! Amount:

_____ Points

Running Total (A through K Quizzes):

_____ Points

Long before there were real estate agents, people were surveying, buying, and selling land. Tell us what you know about these cases.

Answers on next page.

100 Who did God say should have first inheritance rights to the property of a man who died without sons?

200 What did the law forbid Israelites to do to their neighbors' "landmarks," or boundary stones?

300 Which tribe of Israel, set apart to be priests, did not receive part of the Promised Land, since "the Lord is their inheritance"?

400 What field was purchased by the chief priests with the "blood money" they got back from a remorseful Judas Iscariot?

500 What special celebration, every fifty years, saw property that had been sold returned to its original owners?

Land answers

100	his daughters (Numbers 27:1–8)
200	move, or remove, them (Deuteronomy 19:14)
300	the Levites (Joshua 18:3–7)
400	the potter's field (Matthew 27:3–7)
500	Jubilee (Leviticus 25:28)

Your Score for This Quiz:

_____ **Points**

Leviticus

Leviticus is the Old Testament rule book. But you'll also find some stories inside, usually of people who broke those rules. How much do you know about this third book of the Bible?

Answers on next page.

100 What body fluid did God forbid the Israelites to eat because it holds the life of every creature?

200 What was the method of execution for a man who blasphemed the Lord's name with a curse?

300 What is one of the two kinds of birds a poor person could substitute for a lamb when making sacrifice for sin?

400 What term, meaning "one who bears blame," described a sacrificial goat chosen by lot to be set free in the desert?

500 What two sons of Aaron were burned to death for offering unauthorized fire to the Lord?

Leviticus answers

100	blood (Leviticus 17:13–14)
200	stoning (Leviticus 24:10–23)
300	dove or pigeon (Leviticus 5:6–7)
400	scapegoat (Leviticus 16:6–10)
500	Nadab and Abihu (Leviticus 10:1–2)

Your Score for This Quiz:

_____ Points

Cumulative Score, L Quizzes:

_____ Points

Lovely People

Call them the Bible's supermodels. . . . What do you know about these lovely ladies—and one handsome man—from the pages of Scripture?

Answers on next page.

100 What beautiful woman was the wife of Abram, later known as Abraham?

200 What future Israelite leader, as a baby, was described as "no ordinary child" or "exceeding fair" (KJV)?

300 What Old Testament queen was deposed and later replaced by Esther when she refused to parade her beauty at a royal banquet?

400 What beautiful daughter of David was mistreated by her stepbrother Amnon—who paid for that sin with his life?

500 What intelligent and beautiful woman, the wife of the surly Nabal, married King David after Nabal died?

Lovely People answers

100	Sarai, later known as Sarah (Genesis 12:11, 17:15)
200	Moses (Acts 7:20)
300	Vashti (Esther 1:10–19)
400	Tamar (2 Samuel 13:1–14, 28–29)
500	Abigail (1 Samuel 25:3, 39–42)

Your Score for This Quiz:

_____ Points

Cumulative Score, L Quizzes:

_____ Points

Luke

Linus quoted him at length in *The Charlie Brown Christmas Special*. . .not bad for a guy who wrote almost two thousand years ago. What else do you know about the biblical writer Luke?

Answers on next page.

100 What professional title, besides missionary, did Luke hold?

200 What group of people, according to Luke, received the angels' announcement of the birth of Jesus?

300 What young man, who fell from a window and died during a sermon by the apostle Paul, is described in Luke's book of Acts?

400 What are two of the four ways Luke says the young boy Jesus grew up?

500 To whom did Luke address the New Testament books of Luke and Acts?

Luke answers

100	doctor (Colossians 4:14)
200	shepherds (Luke 2:8–15)
300	Eutychus (Acts 20:7–12)
400	in wisdom, stature, favor with God, and favor with men (Luke 2:52)
500	Theophilus (Luke 1:3, Acts 1:1)

Your Score for This Quiz:

_____ Points

Total Score, L Quizzes:

_____ Points

Risk It!

Liberty

The four *L* quizzes are now in the books. . .and it's your opportunity to *Risk It!* How does a category on "Liberty" sound? Consider how much of your total score on the *L* quizzes you want to risk on the one question to follow. If you answer correctly, you add the amount you risked to your total *L* quiz score. . .if you answer incorrectly, you *subtract* the amount you risked. Are you ready? Mark down the amount you're willing to risk, and we'll unveil the question. . . .

Your Total Score, L Quizzes:

_____ Points

Your Risk It! Amount:

_____ Points

What, according to Jesus, would set free the crowds who followed Him?

Answer on next page.

Risk It! answer

the truth (John 8:31–32)

Your Total Score, L Quizzes:

_____ Points

+ or – Your Risk It! Amount:

_____ Points

Running Total (A through L Quizzes):

_____ Points

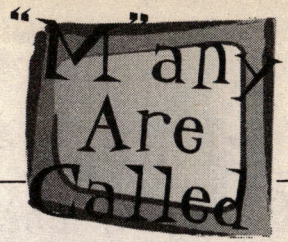

"Many Are Called"

There they are again—the quotation marks in the quiz title. Every answer in this quiz will be a person's name starting with *M*.

Answers on next page.

100 What leader of Israel had a staff, or rod, that turned into a snake?

200 What woman complained when her sister Mary chose to spend time with the visiting Jesus rather than help her with housework?

300 What man, cousin of Queen Esther, served as her advisor and saved the Jews from destruction?

400 What man was chosen by lot to be the twelfth disciple in place of the departed Judas Iscariot?

500 What firstborn son of Joseph received a lesser blessing than his younger brother Ephraim from his grandfather Jacob?

"M"any Are Called answers

100	Moses (Exodus 4:1–4)
200	Martha (Luke 10:38–42)
300	Mordecai (Esther 2:7, 10:3)
400	Matthias (Acts 1:23–26)
500	Manasseh (Genesis 48:17–20)

Your Score for This Quiz:

_____ **Points**

Matthew's Gospel

Most of us already know that there are four Gospels in the New Testament— but what do you know about stories that appear *only* in Matthew's Gospel?

Answers on next page.

100 What visitors, carrying gifts for the young child Jesus, are noted only in Matthew's Gospel?

200 What gem "of great value" did Jesus mention in a parable found only in Matthew's Gospel?

300 What form of suicide used by Judas Iscariot is mentioned only in Matthew's Gospel?

400 What fishing tool did Jesus liken to the kingdom of heaven in a parable found only in Matthew's Gospel?

500 What country did Joseph, Mary, and the baby Jesus flee to for safety from King Herod, in an account found only in Matthew's Gospel?

131

Matthew's Gospel answers

100	Magi, or wise men (Matthew 2:1–2)
200	pearl (Matthew 13:45–46)
300	hanging (Matthew 27:5)
400	a net (Matthew 13:47–50)
500	Egypt (Matthew 2:13)

Your Score for This Quiz:

_____ Points

Cumulative Score, M Quizzes:

_____ Points

Miracles

They don't call them "miracles" for nothing.... Tell us what you know about these amazing stories from the Bible.

Answers on next page.

100 What city's walls fell at the shout of Joshua's army?

200 What did Jesus, in His first recorded miracle, change into wine?

300 In what town did Elijah bring a widow's son back to life?

400 What river divided when the prophet Elisha struck it with Elijah's cloak?

500 What two cloth items, after being touched by the apostle Paul, were used to heal the sick and drive out demons?

Miracles answers

100	Jericho (Joshua 6:2–5, 20)
200	water (John 2:1–11)
300	Zarephath (1 Kings 17:8–22)
400	the Jordan (2 Kings 2:12–14)
500	handkerchiefs and aprons (Acts 19:11–12)

Your Score for This Quiz:

_____ Points

Cumulative Score, M Quizzes:

_____ Points

Mounts and Mountains

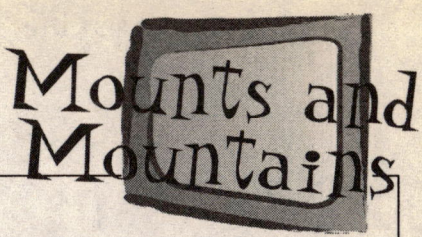

Everest, McKinley, and the Matterhorn don't appear in the Bible, but several other mounts and mountains do. What do you remember about the following?

Answers on next page.

100 What mountain chain was the final stopping point for Noah's ark?

200 What mount is associated with the heavenly Jerusalem?

300 What mountain did Moses climb to see the Promised Land he would not be allowed to enter?

400 What mountain was the setting for Moses' encounter with God in a burning bush?

500 What well-known Bible character died on Mount Hor?

Mounts and Mountains
answers

100	Ararat (Genesis 8:1–4)
200	Zion, or Sion (Hebrews 12:22)
300	Pisgah (Deuteronomy 3:21–29)
400	Horeb (Exodus 3:1–6)
500	Aaron (Numbers 33:39)

Your Score for This Quiz:

_____ **Points**

Total Score, M Quizzes:

_____ **Points**

Risk It!

Magical Moments

We've now reached the *Risk It!* question for the *M* quizzes. . .and "Magical Moments" sounds interesting. Think about how much of your total score on the *M* quizzes you want to risk on the one question following. If you answer correctly, you add the amount you risked to your total *M* quiz score. . .if you answer incorrectly, you *subtract* the amount you risked. Have you determined your number? Write down the amount you're willing to risk, and we'll unveil the question. . . .

Your Total Score, M Quizzes:

_____ Points

Your Risk It! Amount:

_____ Points

What prophet did King Saul have a medium at Endor call up from the dead?

Answer on next page.

Risk It! answer

Samuel (1 Samuel 28:1–15)

Your Total Score, M Quizzes:

_____ Points

+ or – Your Risk It! Amount:

_____ Points

Running Total (A through M Quizzes):

_____ Points

Nighttime

Even before electric lighting, nighttime was a busy time for people in the Bible. What do you know about these nighttime experiences?

Answers on next page.

100 Which day of creation included God making night?

200 What prophet, troubled by King Saul's waywardness, cried out all night long to God?

300 What supernatural source of nighttime light led the Israelites on their journey out of Egypt?

400 Where was Paul, experiencing a nighttime vision of a man, invited to spread the gospel?

500 What sin did the apostle Paul tell the Thessalonians is likely to occur at night?

Nighttime answers

100	the first (Genesis 1:5)
200	Samuel (1 Samuel 15:10–11)
300	a pillar of fire (Exodus 13:18–22)
400	Macedonia (Acts 16:9–10)
500	drunkenness (1 Thessalonians 5:7)

Your Score for This Quiz:

_____ Points

Nineveh

It may have been the New York City of its time—Nineveh was an important place in need of God. . . . Can you recall its story well enough to answer these questions?

Answers on next page.

100 What prophet tried to disobey God's call to preach to Nineveh—and was waylaid by a giant fish?

200 How many days' warning of the destruction to come did God give Nineveh?

300 What mournful clothing did the people of Nineveh wear to show their repentance before God?

400 Of 12,000, 120,000, or 1.2 million, what was the approximate population of what God called the "great city" of Nineveh?

500 What "mighty hunter" built Nineveh shortly after Noah's time?

Nineveh answers

100	Jonah (Jonah 1:1–3, 17)
200	forty (Jonah 3:4)
300	sackcloth (Jonah 3:5)
400	120,000 (Jonah 4:11)
500	Nimrod (Genesis 10:8–11)

Your Score for This Quiz:

_____ Points

Cumulative Score, N Quizzes:

_____ Points

You see those quotation marks around the letter *N*. . .so you know what each answer will begin with. Now get to it!

Answers on next page.

100 Who built an ark to save his family and every type of animal from a worldwide flood?

200 Who did Jesus tell an expert in the Law he should love as himself?

300 What wall-building Jewish exile has a book of the Old Testament named for him?

400 What kind of man was Samson, who was never to cut his hair?

500 What disciple first responded to news of the Messiah by saying, "Nazareth! Can anything good come from there?"

"N" joy answers

100	Noah (Genesis 6)
200	(his) neighbor (Matthew 22:34–39)
300	Nehemiah (Nehemiah 1–2:8)
400	Nazirite (Judges 13)
500	Nathanael (John 1:43–51)

Your Score for This Quiz:

_____ Points

Cumulative Score, N Quizzes:

_____ Points

Number, Number

Have you been keeping count? The Bible is full of numbers. . . . Can you remember these?

Answers on next page.

100 How many days did God use to create the world and everything in it?

200 How many men did Moses send into Canaan to spy out the land?

300 How many days was Lazarus in the grave before being resurrected?

400 What, according to Revelation, is the "number of the beast"?

500 How many silver coins did Judas Iscariot receive for betraying Jesus?

Number, Number answers

100	six (Genesis 1:31–2:1)
200	twelve (Numbers 13:1–15)
300	four (John 11:17)
400	666 (Revelation 13:18)
500	thirty (Matthew 27:3–4)

Your Score for This Quiz:

_____ Points

Total Score, N Quizzes:

_____ Points

Risk It!

New Birth

Well, you've completed all four *N* quizzes and reached the *Risk It!* portion of the game. What do you know about the new birth? Consider how much of your total score on the *N* quizzes you want to risk on the one question following. If you answer correctly, you add the amount you risked to your total *N* quiz score. . .if you answer incorrectly, you *subtract* the amount you risked. Have you made your decision? Mark down the amount you're willing to risk, and we'll unveil the question. . . .

Your Total Score, N Quizzes:

_____ Points

Your Risk It! Amount:

_____ Points

What Jewish ruler was told by Jesus, "You must be born again"?

Answer on next page.

Risk It! answer

Nicodemus (John 3:1–7)

Your Total Score, N Quizzes:

_____ **Points**

+ or – Your Risk It! Amount:

_____ **Points**

Running Total (A through N Quizzes):

_____ **Points**

Occupations

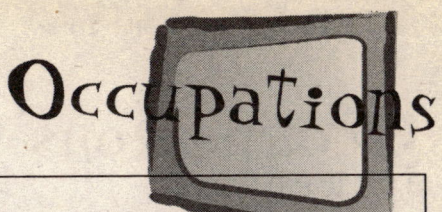

 That's the big word for "jobs"—and Bible people had them just like we do today. Tell us what you know about these ancient occupations.

Answers on next page.

100 What was Matthew's job before he became a disciple of Jesus?

200 What job did the youthful David have before his anointing as king?

300 Who was one of the two royal employees who shared a jail cell with the falsely accused Joseph?

400 What occupation did the apostle Paul have in addition to his missionary duties?

500 What was the occupation of the man Demetrius, a devotee of the goddess Artemis, also known as Diana?

Occupations
answers

100	tax collector (Matthew 9:9)
200	shepherd (1 Samuel 16:11–13)
300	cupbearer (or butler) and baker (Genesis 40)
400	tentmaker (Acts 18:1–3)
500	silversmith (Acts 19:24)

Your Score for This Quiz:

_____ Points

Old People

None of us are getting any younger, you know. What can you recall about the elderly in the Bible?

Answers on next page.

100 What color hair, according to the Proverbs, is the "splendor of the old"?

200 What man lived the longest life recorded in the Bible—969 years?

300 What son of Jared lived "only" 365 years but didn't die—because God took him away?

400 What elderly prophetess met Mary, Joseph, and the baby Jesus at the temple and thanked God for the redemption to come?

500 How old was Noah when God sent the flood to destroy the earth?

Old People answers

100	gray (Proverbs 20:29)
200	Methuselah (Genesis 5:27)
300	Enoch (Genesis 5:18, 23–24, Hebrews 11:5)
400	Anna (Luke 2:36–38)
500	six hundred (Genesis 7:11)

Your Score for This Quiz:

_____ Points

Cumulative Score, 0 Quizzes:

_____ Points

"O" My!

Okay, here's a category where all the answers start with the letter *O*. Onward!

Answers on next page.

100 What "Mount of" was frequented by Jesus?

200 What Greek letter did Jesus pair with "Alpha" to describe Himself?

300 What kind of tree caught Absalom's head as he rode underneath on a mule, leaving him hanging?

400 What did Samuel tell King Saul is better than sacrifice?

500 What widowed woman left her mother-in-law, Naomi, and sister-in-law, Ruth, to return to her home-land of Moab?

"O" My! answers

100	Olives (Luke 22:39)
200	Omega (Revelation 22:12–13)
300	oak (2 Samuel 18:9–10)
400	(to) obey (1 Samuel 15:22–25)
500	Orpah (Ruth 1:3–5, 14–15)

Your Score for This Quiz:

_____ Points

Cumulative Score, O Quizzes:

_____ Points

Once Upon a Rhyme

Yes, this is a silly category. . . . You'll
need to combine two rhyming words to
provide the answers to these questions.

Answers on next page.

100   What did the first woman sew
together to hide her nakedness?

200   What would you call the king of
Israel who stood head and shoulders
above everyone else?

300   What would you call flowers of
Sharon belonging to the Ten
Commandments man?

400   What did the apostle Paul say some
Christians might do to the detriment
of less mature believers?

500   What might you call the flames the
disciple Cephas used to warm himself
the night of Jesus' arrest?

Once Upon a Rhyme answers

100	Eve's leaves (Genesis 3:1–20)
200	Tall Saul (1 Samuel 9:2)
300	Moses' roses (Exodus 20:1–21, Song of Songs 2:1)
400	eat meat (1 Corinthians 8:4–13)
500	Peter's heaters (John 1:42, Luke 22:54–55)

Your Score for This Quiz:

_____ Points

Total Score, O Quizzes:

_____ Points

Onesimus

 All right. . .you've navigated the *O* quizzes and it's time for another *Risk It!* question. How much do you know about Onesimus? Consider how much of your total score on the *O* quizzes you want to risk on the one question following. If you answer correctly, you add the amount you risked to your total *O* quiz score. . .if you answer incorrectly, you *subtract* the amount you risked. Ready to decide? Jot down the amount you're willing to risk, and we'll unveil the question. . . .

Your Total Score, O Quizzes:

_____ Points

Your Risk It! Amount:

_____ Points

What was the relationship of Onesimus to the New Testament letter recipient Philemon?

Answer on next page.

Risk It! answer

slave (Philemon 10–16)

Your Total Score, O Quizzes:

_____ Points

+ or – Your Risk It! Amount:

_____ Points

Running Total (A through O Quizzes):

_____ Points

Passover

The Jews have been commemorating the Passover for thousands of years now. What do you know about its origins?

Answers on next page.

100 What kind of animal did God tell the Israelites to slaughter and eat during the Passover?

200 Where were the Israelites to apply some of the blood from the Passover sacrifice?

300 Who was to die in Egyptian households on the night of Passover?

400 What baking product was banned from Israelite homes for an entire week during the Passover celebration?

500 What was the requirement for male slaves and foreigners to eat the Passover meal?

Passover answers

100	a lamb (Exodus 12:3–6)
200	to their doorframes (Exodus 12:7)
300	the firstborn (Exodus 12:12–13)
400	yeast, or leaven (Exodus 12:19)
500	circumcision (Exodus 12:43–49)

Your Score for This Quiz:

_____ Points

Pharisees

You probably already know that the Pharisees—the religious leaders of the day—had an ongoing battle with Jesus. Can you remember specifics of their conflict?

Answers on next page.

100 What civic duty did the Pharisees hope to use to get Jesus in trouble with Caesar?

200 What short word, meaning "trouble," did Jesus pronounce on the Pharisees seven times in one speech?

300 What did Jesus do on a Sabbath day that so infuriated the Pharisees they began plotting to kill Him?

400 What type of person did Jesus use to contrast with the self-righteous Pharisees in a parable on humility?

500 What did Jesus say the Pharisees would see in response to their demand for a sign from heaven?

Pharisees answers

100	paying taxes (Luke 20:20–26)
200	woe (Matthew 23:13–32)
300	heal (Matthew 12:9–14)
400	a tax collector, or publican (Luke 18:9–14)
500	the sign of Jonah (Matthew 16:1–4)

Your Score for This Quiz:

_____ Points

Cumulative Score, P Quizzes:

_____ Points

Pontius Pilate

The perfect politician—Pilate said he could find no fault in Jesus, but allowed Him to be crucified anyway. What else do you know about this Roman official?

Answers on next page.

100 What symbolic act did Pontius Pilate perform to try to brush aside responsibility for Jesus' crucifixion?

200 What position of authority did Pontius Pilate hold?

300 Who urged Pontius Pilate to leave Jesus alone after having a dream about Him?

400 What three-word question did Pontius Pilate utter after Jesus said He had come into the world to testify to the truth?

500 What fellow government official— formerly an enemy—became Pontius Pilate's friend during Jesus' trial?

Pontius Pilate answers

100	He washed his hands (Matthew 27:24)
200	governor (Matthew 27:2)
300	Pilate's wife (Matthew 27:19)
400	"What is truth?" (John 18:37–38)
500	Herod (Luke 23:5–12)

Your Score for This Quiz:

_____ Points

Cumulative Score, P Quizzes:

_____ Points

 You don't have to be an accountant to understand the Bible's system of profit and loss. Can you add to your score by answering these five questions?

Answers on next page.

100 What did the apostle Paul say is profitable, or useful, for teaching, rebuking, correcting, and training in righteousness?

200 What did Jesus say a man could forfeit, negating the gain of "the whole world"?

300 What, along with godliness, did the apostle Paul tell Timothy "is great gain"?

400 Whose loss, according to the book of Romans, meant "riches" for the Gentiles?

500 How did Paul describe everything he had lost in his life in his efforts to gain Christ?

Profit and Loss answers

100	Scripture (2 Timothy 3:16)
200	his soul (Mark 8:36)
300	contentment (1 Timothy 6:6)
400	Israel (Romans 11:7–12)
500	rubbish, or dung (Philippians 3:7–8)

Your Score for This Quiz:

_____ **Points**

Total Score, P Quizzes:

_____ **Points**

Risk It!

Psalms

Congratulations—you've reached the *Risk It!* section for the *P* quizzes. Feel confident on the Psalms? Decide how much of your total score on the *P* quizzes you want to risk on the one question to follow. If you answer correctly, you add the amount you risked to your total *P* quiz score. . .if you answer incorrectly, you *subtract* the amount you risked. Made your decision? Write down the amount you're willing to risk, and we'll unveil the question. . . .

Your Total Score, P Quizzes:

_____ Points

Your Risk It! Amount:

_____ Points

What did the psalmist say God's words, or promises, are sweeter than?

Answer on next page.

Risk It! answer

honey (Psalm 119:103)

Your Total Score, P Quizzes:

_____ Points

+ or – Your Risk It! Amount:

_____ Points

Running Total (A through P Quizzes):

_____ Points

There aren't a lot of "*Q* words" in the Bible. . .but there are enough to fill this category. What's your Bible IQ?

Answers on next page.

100 What ruler of Sheba, intrigued by reports of Solomon's wisdom, paid a visit to test Solomon with hard questions?

200 What arrow-carrying case did the psalmist liken to a man with many sons?

300 What kind of bird did God miraculously provide for the Israelites, who had grown tired of manna?

400 What adjective, besides "peaceful," describes the kind of Christian life Paul told Timothy to live?

500 How did Jesus instruct Judas Iscariot to do his evil work of betrayal?

"Q" It Up answers

1OO	queen (1 Kings 10:1)
2OO	quiver (Psalm 127:4–5)
3OO	quail (Numbers 11:31–32)
4OO	quiet (1 Timothy 2:1–2)
5OO	quickly (John 13:27)

Your Score for This Quiz:

_____ Points

Quenching

You don't often hear the word "quench" used in everyday speech. . .but it's a prominent word in the Bible. Tell us what you know about it.

Answers on next page.

100 What terrible locale, according to Jesus, is a place where "the fire is not quenched"?

200 What did the apostle Paul warn the Thessalonians against quenching—or putting out its fire?

300 What piece of the armor of God can quench the fiery darts or flaming arrows of Satan?

400 What, according to the Song of Songs, cannot quench love?

500 What captain in Deborah's army is listed in Hebrews as a hero of faith, among those who "quenched the fury of the flames"?

Quenching answers

100	hell (Mark 9:45–48)
200	the Spirit (1 Thessalonians 5:19)
300	the shield of faith (Ephesians 6:16)
400	many waters (Song of Songs 8:7)
500	Barak (Judges 4:14–15, Hebrews 11:32–34)

Your Score for This Quiz:

_____ Points

Cumulative Score, Q Quizzes:

_____ Points

Questions

Here are some questions about questions. But the real question is, "Do you have answers?"

Answers on next page.

100 Who did Jesus say He was calling to repentance when Pharisees asked why He ate with disreputable people?

200 What "visual aid" did Jesus use to answer the disciples' question, "Who is the greatest in the kingdom of heaven?"

300 What imprisoned preacher sent his own disciples to Jesus to ask if He was the expected Messiah?

400 What answer did Jesus give to an expert in the law who asked which commandment was greatest?

500 What two-part answer did Jesus give to trouble-making Pharisees who asked Him whether they should pay taxes to Caesar?

Questions answers

100	sinners (Matthew 9:10–13)
200	a child (Matthew 18:1–4)
300	John the Baptist (Matthew 11:1–15)
400	"Love the Lord your God with all your heart and with all your soul and with all your mind." (Matthew 22:34–40)
500	"Give to Caesar what is Caesar's and to God what is God's." (Mark 12:13–17)

Your Score for This Quiz:

_____ Points

Cumulative Score, Q Quizzes:

_____ Points

Quickly!

This is a quiz about the quick. What do you know about Bible characters and things that go fast?

Answers on next page.

100 Which disciple, according to Luke, ran to Jesus' tomb after faithful women told him of the Lord's resurrection?

200 What phrases describe the time frame in which Christians will be changed at the sound of the last trumpet?

300 What prostitute urged the men of Jericho to quickly pursue two Israelite spies—while she harbored those spies in her own home?

400 What prophet summoned fire from heaven to destroy fifty-one soldiers carrying King Ahaziah's command to "Come down at once!"?

500 What king of Israel was known for his furious chariot driving—likened to the driving of "a madman"?

Quickly! answers

100	Peter (Luke 24:1–12)
200	"in a flash, in the twinkling of an eye" (1 Corinthians 15:52)
300	Rahab (Joshua 2:1–6)
400	Elijah (2 Kings 1:1–12)
500	Jehu (2 Kings 9:2–3, 20)

Your Score for This Quiz:

_____ Points

Total Score, 0, Quizzes:

_____ Points

Risk It!

Quarrelsome People

The *Q* questions are history. . .now it's time to *Risk It!* What do you know about quarrelsome people in the Bible? Choose how much of your total score on the *Q* quizzes you want to risk on the one question following. If you answer correctly, you add the amount you risked to your total *Q* quiz score. . .if you answer incorrectly, you *subtract* the amount you risked. Made up your mind yet? Note the amount you're willing to risk, and we'll unveil the question. . . .

Your Total Score, Q Quizzes:

_____ Points

Your Risk It! Amount:

_____ Points

Where did Moses obtain water for the quarreling Israelites at a dry place called Kadesh?

Answer on next page.

Risk It! answer

from a rock (Numbers 20:1–11)

Your Total Score, Q, Quizzes:

_____ Points

+ or – Your Risk It! Amount:

_____ Points

Running Total (A through Q Quizzes):

_____ Points

Riches of Earth

No, this isn't a quiz about guys named Rich. We're talking money, moolah, dinero. . .and what the Bible says about it. Put your money where your mouth is, and tell us what you know.

Answers on next page.

100 What feeling toward money is "a root of all kinds of evil"?

200 What two things, according to Jesus, destroy treasures on earth?

300 What coming day, according to the Proverbs, shows the worthlessness of wealth?

400 What dishonest quality of wealth, according to Jesus' parable of the sower, causes some Christians to be unfruitful?

500 What word did the apostle Paul use to describe wealth or riches in his first letter to Timothy?

Riches of Earth
answers

100	love (1 Timothy 6:10)
200	moth and rust (Matthew 6:19)
300	the day of wrath (Proverbs 11:4)
400	deceitfulness (Matthew 13:22)
500	uncertain (1 Timothy 6:17)

Your Score for This Quiz:

_____ Points

Rivers

You won't find the Mississippi or the Amazon in the Bible, but several other rivers are noted. What do you recall of them?

Answers on next page.

100 What future leader of Israel, as a three-month-old baby, was placed in a basket in the river of Egypt—the Nile?

200 What form did the Holy Spirit take when it descended on Jesus after His baptism in the Jordan River?

300 Of the four rivers that were said to flow from the Garden of Eden, what two share names with important rivers of the modern Middle East?

400 What leprous army commander, told to wash in the Jordan for healing, preferred to wash in the Abana or Pharpar rivers of his homeland?

500 Where does "the river of the water of life" in the new Jerusalem originate?

Rivers answers

100	Moses (Exodus 2:1–10)
200	a dove (Matthew 3:13–17)
300	Tigris and Euphrates (Genesis 2:10–14)
400	Naaman (2 Kings 5:10–14)
500	the throne of God (Revelation 22:1–2)

Your Score for This Quiz:

_____ Points

Cumulative Score, R Quizzes:

_____ Points

Ruth's story

Looking for a little romance? Try the Bible's story of Ruth—that's where the questions in this quiz come from.

Answers on next page.

100 What great-grandson of Ruth became the most prominent king of Israel?

200 What was Ruth doing the first time she saw Boaz, the man she would marry?

300 What role did Boaz play by marrying Ruth and purchasing the property of her former in-laws?

400 What was the name of Ruth's first husband, who died?

500 What name, meaning "Bitter," did Ruth's newly-widowed mother-in-law give herself?

Ruth's Story answers

100	David (Ruth 4:13–17)
200	gleaning (Ruth 2:5–8)
300	kinsman-redeemer (Ruth 3:7–13)
400	Mahlon (Ruth 4:10)
500	Mara (Ruth 1:20)

Your Score for This Quiz:

_____ Points

Cumulative Score, R Quizzes:

_____ Points

You noticed the quotation marks? Then you already know that every answer in this quiz begins with the letter *R*.

Answers on next page.

100 What did Jesus say He came to call sinners to?

200 What daughter of Bethuel was wife of the patriarch Isaac?

300 What kind of lion does the apostle Peter compare the devil to?

400 What name—also the name of a bay in Delaware—did Isaac give to a well he dug?

500 What kind of fire does the prophet Malachi say the Lord will be like in the day of judgment?

"R" You Sure?
answers

100	repentance (Luke 5:31–32)
200	Rebekah (Genesis 25:20)
300	roaring (1 Peter 5:8)
400	Rehoboth (Genesis 26:22)
500	refiner's (Malachi 3:1–2)

Your Score for This Quiz:

_____ Points

Total Score, R Quizzes:

_____ Points

Risk It!

Revenge

And now you can *Risk It!* for the four *R* quizzes—as we test your knowledge of the category "Revenge." Consider how much of your total score on the *R* quizzes you want to risk on the one question to follow. If you answer correctly, you add the amount you risked to your total *R* quiz score. . .if you answer incorrectly, you *subtract* the amount you risked. Settled on a number? Write down the amount you're willing to risk, and we'll unveil the question. . . .

Your Total Score, R Quizzes:

_____ Points

Your Risk It! Amount:

_____ Points

What three words complete God's promise, "It is mine to avenge; . . ." quoted by Paul in his letter to the Romans?

Answer on next page.

Risk It! answer

"I will repay" (Romans 12:19)

Your Total Score, R Quizzes:

_____ Points

+ or – Your Risk It! Amount:

_____ Points

Running Total (A through R Quizzes):

_____ Points

Salt

Salt—chemical compound NaCl—was pretty important stuff in the Bible. Tell us what you know about salt, both literal and figurative.

Answers on next page.

100 Whose wife was turned into a pillar of salt for looking back on the doomed cities of Sodom and Gomorrah?

200 What did Jesus tell His disciples they were "the salt of"?

300 What did the apostle Paul say should be "seasoned with salt"?

400 What did Mark quote Jesus as saying everyone would be "salted with"?

500 What Old Testament prophet healed the waters of Jericho by throwing salt into a spring?

Salt answers

100	Lot (Genesis 19:23–26)
200	the earth (Matthew 5:13)
300	conversation, or speech (Colossians 4:6)
400	fire (Mark 9:49)
500	Elisha (2 Kings 2:19–22)

Your Score for This Quiz:

_____ Points

Simon was a popular name in Bible times. Here are five men who were known by the name Simon—your job is to more clearly identify each one.

Answers on next page.

100 What did a Simon from Cyrene carry for Jesus as He walked to His execution?

200 What famous half-brother could a certain Simon, with his full brothers James, Joseph, and Judas, claim?

300 What two-word nickname—from a dreaded disease he had—described a Simon from Bethany?

400 What forbidden art did a Simon from Samaria practice before he accepted Christ?

500 What job was held by a Simon from Joppa, who entertained the apostle Peter in his house by the sea?

Simon Who?
answers

100	His cross (Luke 23:26)
200	Jesus (Matthew 13:53–56)
300	"the Leper" (Mark 14:3)
400	sorcery (Acts 8:9–24)
500	tanner (Acts 10:30–33)

Your Score for This Quiz:

_____ Points

Cumulative Score, 5 Quizzes:

_____ Points

"Sons of Men"

Two hints on this quiz: Every answer begins with the letter *S*, and each answer is the name of a biblical man.

Answers on next page.

100 What man is generally listed first in the accounts of Noah's sons?

200 What man, described in Acts as "full of faith and of the Holy Spirit," was one of seven chosen to relieve the apostles of waiting on tables?

300 What devout man held the baby Jesus when Mary and Joseph presented Him at the temple?

400 What king of Assyria insulted God to King Hezekiah of Judah—and paid for it with his life?

500 What man, a Horonite, opposed Nehemiah and the Jews rebuilding the walls of Jerusalem?

"S"ons of Men
answers

100	Shem (Genesis 5:32)
200	Stephen (Acts 6:1–5)
300	Simeon (Luke 2:25–32)
400	Sennacherib (2 Kings 19:5–13, 35–37)
500	Sanballat (Nehemiah 2:10, 4:1–2)

Your Score for This Quiz:

_____ Points

Cumulative Score, S Quizzes:

_____ Points

Soul Winners

Call it "evangelism," "preaching the gospel," or "bringing in the sheaves." Christians have an obligation to win souls. What do you recall about the Bible's soul-winning passages?

Answers on next page.

100   What two disciples from Jesus' inner circle, described as "unschooled, ordinary men," amazed the Jewish leaders with their courage in preaching the gospel?

200   What agricultural term did Jesus use to describe the soul-winners' goal?

300   What businesswoman from Thyatira, a seller of purple cloth, became a Christian after hearing Paul share the gospel?

400   What word did Solomon, in the Proverbs, use to describe soul winners?

500   What five-word phrase did the apostle Paul say he had become in his efforts to bring various people to Christ?

Soul Winners
answers

100	Peter and John (Acts 4:1–20)
200	harvest (Luke 10:1–2)
300	Lydia (Acts 16:13–15)
400	wise (Proverbs 11:30)
500	"all things to all men" (1 Corinthians 9:22)

Your Score for This Quiz:

_____ Points

Total Score, 5 Quizzes:

_____ Points

Risk It!

Satan's Schemes

Well, you've gone through all four *S* quizzes and reached the *Risk It!* portion of the game. Let's test your knowledge of Satan's schemes in the Bible. Think over how much of your total score on the *S* quizzes you want to risk on the one question following. If you answer correctly, you add the amount you risked to your total *S* quiz score. . .if you answer incorrectly, you *subtract* the amount you risked. Have you decided? Mark down the amount you're willing to risk, and we'll unveil the question. . . .

Your Total Score, S Quizzes:

_____ Points

Your Risk It! Amount:

_____ Points

How many days had Jesus fasted in the desert when Satan tempted Him to turn stones into bread?

Answer on next page.

Risk It! answer

---

forty (Matthew 4:1–4)

Your Total Score, S Quizzes:

_____ Points

+ or – Your Risk It! Amount:

_____ Points

Running Total (A through S Quizzes):

_____ Points

Tithes and Offerings

The apostle Paul quoted Jesus as saying "It is more blessed to give than to receive." What do you know about the Bible's instruction on tithes and offerings?

Answers on next page.

100 What attitude of giving, according to the apostle Paul, does God love?

200 Which day of the week did the apostle Paul tell believers to put aside money for their offerings?

300 What two words describe the woman Jesus commended for giving an offering of two small copper coins—or "mites"?

400 What priest of Salem received a tithe from the patriarch Abram, later called Abraham?

500 What three spices did Jesus scold Pharisees for tithing while neglecting more important issues like justice and mercy?

Tithes and Offerings answers

100	cheerful (2 Corinthians 9:7)
200	the first day (1 Corinthians 16:2)
300	"poor widow" (Mark 12:41–43)
400	Melchizedek (Genesis 14:18–20)
500	mint, dill (or anise), and cummin (Matthew 23:23)

Your Score for This Quiz:

_____ **Points**

Tombs

Yeah, we're talking about tombs—those places that hold dead bodies. You'll find quite a few of them in Scripture. . . .
What do you remember about these?

Answers on next page.

100 Whose tomb was marked by a pillar erected by her husband, Jacob?

200 What kind of tomb did Jesus derisively use to describe the hypocritical Pharisees and teachers of the law?

300 Who gave up his own new tomb for the burial of the crucified Jesus?

400 What Old Testament woman was buried in a cave in the field of Machpelah?

500 What son and grandson of Kish were reburied in his tomb after their deaths in battle?

Tombs answers

100	Rachel (Genesis 35:19–20)
200	whitewashed, or whited (Matthew 23:27–28)
300	Joseph of Arimathea (Matthew 27:57–60)
400	Sarah (Genesis 23:19)
500	Saul and Jonathan (2 Samuel 21:13–14)

Your Score for This Quiz:

_____ **Points**

Cumulative Score, T Quizzes:

_____ **Points**

Trees

They didn't have Arbor Day, but they did have plenty of trees. Show us your knowledge of these trees of the Bible.

Answers on next page.

100 What kind of tree did a man named Zacchaeus climb in order to see Jesus?

200 What type of tree immediately withered when Jesus cursed it—an event Jesus used to teach His disciples about faith?

300 What famous tree of Lebanon was used by the psalmist as a metaphor for the righteous?

400 What kind of tree was Gideon working under when the angel of the Lord greeted him?

500 What type of tree does the love-smitten woman of the Song of Songs compare her man to?

Trees answers

100	sycamore-fig (Luke 19:1–4)
200	fig (Matthew 21:18–22)
300	cedar (Psalm 92:12)
400	oak (Judges 6:11–12)
500	apple (Song of Songs 2:3)

Your Score for This Quiz:

_____ Points

Cumulative Score, T Quizzes:

_____ Points

"T" Time

Another set of quotation marks, and another tip-off to aid you: All of the following answers will begin with the letter *T*.

Answers on next page.

100 What troublesome desire did Paul say is "common to man"?

200 What city was the birthplace of the apostle Paul?

300 Where did Abraham find a ram to sacrifice after God stopped him from sacrificing his son Isaac?

400 What two *T*s grew from the ground God cursed after Adam and Eve's sin?

500 Which of the churches of Revelation did Jesus criticize for tolerating "that woman Jezebel"?

"T" Time answers

100	temptation (1 Corinthians 10:13)
200	Tarsus (Acts 22:2–3)
300	thicket (Genesis 22:9–13)
400	thorns and thistles (Genesis 3:17–18)
500	Thyatira (Revelation 2:18–20)

Your Score for This Quiz:

_____ Points

Total Score, T Quizzes:

_____ Points

Risk It!

Thomas

It's time to *Risk It!* for the *T* quizzes. What do you know about Thomas? Think about how much of your total score on the *T* quizzes you want to risk on the one question following. If you answer correctly, you add the amount you risked to your total *T* quiz score. . .if you answer incorrectly, you *subtract* the amount you risked. Got your number? Mark down the amount you're willing to risk, and we'll unveil the question. . . .

Your Total Score, T Quizzes:

_____ Points

Your Risk It! Amount:

_____ Points

What second name was Thomas known by?

Answer on next page.

Risk It! answer

Didymus (John 11:16)

Your Total Score, T Quizzes:

_____ Points

+ or – Your Risk It! Amount:

_____ Points

Running Total (A through T Quizzes):

_____ Points

We've called out the letter *U* in the title to this quiz. That lets you know the first letter of each answer.

Answers on next page.

100   In what kind of room did Jesus celebrate His last Passover with His disciples?

200   What, along with wisdom, does Solomon urge readers of the Proverbs to get?

300   What land did the patriarch Abraham hail from?

400   What kind of god had the people of Athens built an altar to—prompting the apostle Paul to share the true God with them?

500   What man, attempting to steady the ark of the covenant on its cart, was struck dead for touching it?

"U" Know?
answers

100	upper (Mark 14:12–15)
200	understanding (Proverbs 4:5–7)
300	Ur of the Chaldeans (Genesis 15:7–8)
400	unknown (Acts 17:22–23)
500	Uzzah (2 Samuel 6:6–7)

Your Score for This Quiz:

_____ Points

Unto Us a Child Is Born

The birth of Christ—a remarkable fulfillment of prophecy and a key event in all human history. What do you remember of the Bible's Christmas story?

Answers on next page.

100 What town in Judea was the birthplace of Jesus?

200 What animal feeding trough served as a temporary bed for the newborn Jesus?

300 What name, meaning "God with us," did Isaiah prophesy for Jesus?

400 What relative did Jesus' mother, Mary, stay with while she was expecting?

500 What, according to the prophet Isaiah, would Jesus carry on His shoulders?

Unto Us a Child Is Born answers

100	Bethlehem (Matthew 2:1)
200	a manger (Luke 2:7)
300	Immanuel or Emmanuel (Isaiah 7:14, Matthew 1:22–23)
400	Elizabeth (Luke 1:36, 56)
500	the government (Isaiah 9:6)

Your Score for This Quiz:

_____ Points

Cumulative Score, U Quizzes:

_____ Points

Uproars

Call 'em riots, hubbubs, or donnybrooks, you'll find a number of uproars in the pages of Scripture! What can you tell us about these?

Answers on next page.

100 What idol were the Israelites worshiping with shouting and singing when Moses arrived with God's Ten Commandments?

200 What disciple was martyred by an angry, screaming crowd, after a critical speech to the Sanhedrin?

300 What did Moses fear the thirsty Israelites would do to him at a dry place called Rephidim?

400 In what city did silversmiths—fearing the effect of Paul's preaching on their idol-making business—stir up a riot?

500 What two groups of people, according to the crowd at Jesus' crucifixion, should bear responsibility for Jesus' death?

Uproars answers

100	the golden calf (Exodus 32:1–4, 17–20)
200	Stephen (Acts 7:51–60)
300	stone him (Exodus 17:1–4)
400	Ephesus (Acts 19:25–32)
500	"us and. . .our children" (Matthew 27:25)

Your Score for This Quiz:

_____ **Points**

Cumulative Score, U Quizzes:

_____ **Points**

Uriah the Hittite

He had a beautiful wife—and that got him killed. What else do you recall of the story of Uriah the Hittite?

Answers on next page.

100 What beautiful wife of Uriah was improperly taken—and made pregnant—by a lustful King David?

200 What was Uriah's occupation?

300 How many nights did David try to make Uriah go home to sleep with his wife?

400 Where did King David later order Uriah?

500 What prophet confronted David about his sins toward Uriah?

Uriah the Hittite
answers

100   Bathsheba (2 Samuel 11:2–5)

200   soldier (2 Samuel 11:7)

300   two (2 Samuel 11:8–13)

400   the fiercest part of the battle, to his death (2 Samuel 11:14–15)

500   Nathan (2 Samuel 12:1–10)

Your Score for This Quiz:

_____ **Points**

Total Score, U Quizzes:

_____ **Points**

Risk It!

Unclean! Unclean!

It's time to *Risk It!* for the *U* quizzes. What do you know about those dramatic words, "Unclean! Unclean!"? Think about how much of your total score on the *U* quizzes you want to risk on the one question following. If you answer correctly, you add the amount you risked to your total *U* quiz score. . .if you answer incorrectly, you *subtract* the amount you risked. Got your number? Mark down the amount you're willing to risk, and we'll unveil the question. . . .

Your Total Score, U Quizzes:

_____ **Points**

Your Risk It! Amount:

_____ **Points**

How many leprous men came to Jesus requesting a mass healing—for which only one returned to praise God?

Answer on next page.

Risk It! answer

ten (Luke 17:11–19)

Your Total Score, U Quizzes:

_____ Points

+ or – Your Risk It! Amount:

_____ Points

Running Total (A through U Quizzes):

_____ Points

Victory and Defeat

You win some, you lose some. . . . *You* could be a winner, depending on how much you know about biblical victories and defeats.

Answers on next page.

100 What weapon did the young David use to fell the giant warrior Goliath?

200 What hostile army, pursuing the people of Israel, was completely destroyed in the middle of the Red Sea?

300 What, according to 1 Corinthians, will be "swallowed up in victory" at the last trumpet?

400 What three-word phrase did Paul use to describe believers who may suffer persecution, famine, and danger—but who are never separated from the love of Christ?

500 What miracle occurred in the heavens the day Joshua and the Israelites defeated the armies of the five kings of the Amorites?

Victory and Defeat answers

100	a sling (1 Samuel 17:4, 50)
200	the Egyptians (Exodus 14:21–28)
300	death (1 Corinthians 15:51–54)
400	"more than conquerors" (Romans 8:35–39)
500	the sun stood still (Joshua 10:9–14)

Your Score for This Quiz:

_____ Points

 No, not the sports car by Dodge. . . we're talking about the slithering, sneaky, snaky kind of viper. Do you remember these stories?

Answers on next page.

100 What religious group did Jesus twice call a "brood (or generation) of vipers"?

200 What Egyptian leader disregarded Moses and Aaron's miracle of turning a staff into a snake?

300 What forbidden tree in the Garden of Eden did the serpent convince Eve to eat from?

400 What metal did Moses use to fashion a snake image that healed Israelites bitten by venomous serpents?

500 What sparkling substance does the writer of Proverbs compare to the poison of a viper?

Vipers answers

100	the Pharisees (Matthew 12:24–34, 23:29–33)
200	Pharaoh (Exodus 7:10–13)
300	the tree of the knowledge of good and evil (Genesis 2:15–17, 3:1–6)
400	bronze, or brass (Numbers 21:4–9)
500	wine (Proverbs 23:31–32)

Your Score for This Quiz:

_____ Points

Cumulative Score, V Quizzes:

_____ Points

Visions appear throughout the Bible—both Old Testament and New. Can you recall details of these five?

Answers on next page.

100 What suffering Old Testament saint complained that God would "terrify" him with visions?

200 What apostle had a vision of animals being let down from heaven in a sheet—and realized God had offered salvation to the Gentiles?

300 What Israelite leader did God speak with face to face rather than in visions?

400 How many golden lamp stands, each representing a church in Asia Minor, did John see in his vision of the Revelation of Christ?

500 What two animals appeared in a prophetic vision of Daniel's, near the Ulai Canal?

Visions answers

100	Job (Job 7:13–14)
200	Peter (Acts 11:1–18)
300	Moses (Numbers 12:6–8)
400	seven (Revelation 1:12–20)
500	ram and goat (Daniel 8:1–12)

Your Score for This Quiz:

_____ Points

Cumulative Score, V Quizzes:

_____ Points

Voice of God

When God speaks, you'd better listen! Were you paying attention when God spoke in these Bible passages?

Answers on next page.

100 What storm-related phenomenon is likened to God's voice in the books of Job and John?

200 Where was the persecutor Saul going when he was stopped on the road and converted by the voice of Jesus?

300 What excuse did Adam give for hiding when he heard God's voice?

400 What two Old Testament figures appeared at Jesus' transfiguration, when God's voice was heard saying, "This is my Son, whom I love; with him I am well pleased"?

500 What three-word title, later applied to Jesus Christ, did the voice of God use to address the prophet Ezekiel?

Voice of God
answers

100	thunder (Job 37:4–5; John 12:23–29)
200	Damascus (Acts 9:1–6)
300	afraid, naked (either answer acceptable) (Genesis 3:9–10)
400	Moses and Elijah (Matthew 17:1–5)
500	"son of man" (Ezekiel 2:1; Matthew 8:20)

Your Score for This Quiz:

_____ Points

Total Score, V Quizzes:

_____ Points

Risk It!

Vows

All right. . .you've completed the *V* quizzes, and it's time to *Risk It!* How confident are you on the category "Vows"? Consider how much of your total score on the *V* quizzes you want to risk on the one question following. If you answer correctly, you add the amount you risked to your total *V* quiz score. . .if you answer incorrectly, you *subtract* the amount you risked. Are you ready? Write down the amount you're willing to risk, and we'll unveil the question. . . .

Your Total Score, V Quizzes:

_____ Points

Your Risk It! Amount:

_____ Points

What judge of Israel made a foolish vow that cost him the life of his only daughter?

Answer on next page.

Risk It! answer

Jephthah (Judges 11:30–39)

Your Total Score, V Quizzes:

_____ Points

+ or – Your Risk It! Amount:

_____ Points

Running Total (A through V Quizzes):

_____ Points

Wisdom

It seems in short supply in today's world, but the Bible is packed with words of wisdom. How wise will you be when it comes to these questions?

Answers on next page.

100 What precious metal, according to Proverbs, cannot compare to the value of wisdom?

200 What does Proverbs say is the "beginning of wisdom"?

300 To whom, according to Proverbs, does a man who loves wisdom bring joy?

400 What relative do the Proverbs say a young man should call wisdom?

500 According to Proverbs, what does the person who gets wisdom love?

Wisdom answers

100	gold (Proverbs 16:16)
200	the fear of the Lord (Proverbs 9:10)
300	his father (Proverbs 29:3)
400	sister (Proverbs 7:4)
500	his own soul (Proverbs 19:8)

Your Score for This Quiz:

_____ Points

Wives

Wives in the Bible come in all varieties—good, bad, and indifferent. What can you recall about these?

Answers on next page.

100 What great patriarch took a wife named Keturah after his first wife died?

200 How many wives did Solomon have—in addition to his three hundred concubines?

300 What daughter of King Saul became the wife of David—for the price of two hundred dead Philistines?

400 Which apostle's wife accompanied him on ministry trips, according to Paul?

500 What second wife of Elkanah provoked his other wife, Hannah, over her barrenness?

Wives answers

100	Abraham (Genesis 25:1)
200	seven hundred (1 Kings 11:1–3)
300	Michal (1 Samuel 18:26–27)
400	Peter, or Cephas (1 Corinthians 9:5)
500	Peninnah (1 Samuel 1:1–6)

Your Score for This Quiz:

_____ **Points**

Cumulative Score, W Quizzes:

_____ **Points**

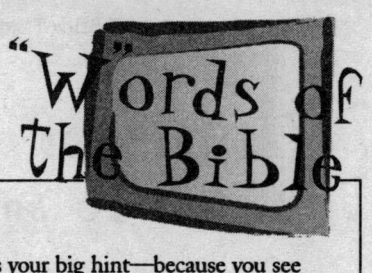

"Words of the Bible"

Here's your big hint—because you see quotation marks in the quiz title, all of the answers will begin with the letter *W.*

Answers on next page.

100 What did God use to take the prophet Elijah into heaven?

200 What word is paired with "signs" to describe the miraculous doings of the apostles after Pentecost?

300 What ravenous animal would feed peacefully with the lamb in the new earth prophesied by Isaiah?

400 What did the patriarch Jacob do all night with God at a place called Peniel?

500 What is the name of the star that falls to earth and poisons a third of the water, as described in Revelation?

"W"ords of the Bible answers

100	whirlwind (2 Kings 2:1)
200	wonders (Acts 5:12)
300	wolf (Isaiah 65:25)
400	wrestle (Genesis 32:22–30)
500	Wormwood (Revelation 8:10–11)

Your Score for This Quiz:

_____ Points

Cumulative Score, W Quizzes:

_____ Points

Workers

You've worked your way through most of the alphabet, to a quiz about "workers." Give your memory a good workout, and try to answer these questions.

Answers on next page.

100 What word did Jesus use to describe the workers compared to the "plentiful" harvest of souls?

200 What did the apostle Paul, writing to the Thessalonians, say that those who refused to work should be kept from doing?

300 What man, who once deserted Paul's mission work in Pamphylia, did the apostle later call "helpful" and ask Timothy to bring to him?

400 What did Jesus once say a worker was worthy of?

500 What word did the writer of Ecclesiastes use to describe the sleep of a laborer?

Workers answers

100	few (Luke 10:2)
200	eating (2 Thessalonians 3:10)
300	(John) Mark (Acts 15:37–38, 2 Timothy 4:11)
400	his wages, or hire (Luke 10:7)
500	sweet (Ecclesiastes 5:12)

Your Score for This Quiz:

_____ Points

Total Score, W Quizzes:

_____ Points

Risk It!

Write a Letter

Here we are at the *Risk It!* category for the four *W* quizzes. Let's test your knowledge in the category "Write a Letter." Decide how much of your total score on the *W* quizzes you want to risk on the one question following. If you answer correctly, you add the amount you risked to your total *W* quiz score. . .if you answer incorrectly, you *subtract* the amount you risked. Have a figure in mind? Mark down the amount you're willing to risk, and we'll unveil the question. . . .

Your Total Score, W Quizzes:

_____ Points

Your Risk It! Amount:

_____ Points

What special prisoner was the subject of a letter from Claudius Lysias to Governor Felix?

Answer on next page.

Risk It! answer

the apostle Paul (Acts 23:25–31)

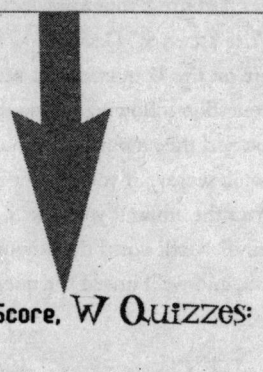

Your Total Score, W Quizzes:

_____ Points

+ or – Your Risk It! Amount:

_____ Points

Running Total (A through W Quizzes):

_____ Points

X at the End

Words starting with *X* are relatively uncommon. . .but it's not unusual to find words *ending* with *X*. Don't worry, you can handle this quiz—relax!

Answers on next page.

100 What did Jesus and Peter pay with a coin found in a fish's mouth?

200 What animal were the Israelites not to muzzle as it was treading grain?

300 What melting substance did the psalmist say his heart had turned to?

400 What metal tool miraculously floated for the prophet Elisha?

500 What Egyptian crop was destroyed by the plague of hail called down by Moses?

X at the End
answers

100	tax (Matthew 17:24–27)
200	ox (Deuteronomy 25:4)
300	wax (Psalm 22:14)
400	ax (2 Kings 6:1–7)
500	flax (Exodus 9:29–31)

Your Score for This Quiz:

_____ **Points**

Xenophobia

According to the dictionary, *xenophobia* is a fear and hatred of foreigners—and something God actually encouraged to keep His chosen people pure. What do you know about these five cases?

Answers on next page.

100 What did the patriarch Isaac forbid his son Jacob to do with a Canaanite woman?

200 What annual ritual dinner of the Israelites were foreigners forbidden to eat?

300 What charge for borrowed money could Israelites apply to foreigners but not to fellow Jews?

400 What nationality, hated by the Jews, provided the "good guy" character in Jesus' parable of a man beaten by robbers?

500 What type of agreement did God forbid between Israel and the nations He would drive out of the Promised Land?

Xenophobia
answers

100	marry (Genesis 28:1)
200	Passover (Exodus 12:43)
300	interest, or usury (Deuteronomy 23:19–20)
400	Samaritan (Luke 10:25–37)
500	treaty, or covenant (Deuteronomy 7:1–2)

Your Score for This Quiz:

_____ Points

Cumulative Score, X Quizzes:

_____ Points

 He's also known as Ahasuerus. . .which is probably a good reason to go by "Xerxes." Tell us what you know about this ancient king.

Answers on next page.

100 What beautiful young Jewish woman was the second queen of the Persian King Xerxes?

200 What modern-day nation, with its capital at New Delhi, marked the eastern extent of King Xerxes's nation?

300 Who discovered and foiled a plot to assassinate King Xerxes?

400 What would King Xerxes hold out to show favor to the people who pleased him?

500 What city was the site of King Xerxes's royal citadel?

Xerxes answers

100	Esther (Esther 2:16–17)
200	India (Esther 8:9)
300	Mordecai (Esther 2:21–23)
400	a golden scepter (Esther 4:11, 5:2)
500	Susa, or Shushan (Esther 1:2)

Your Score for This Quiz:

_____ **Points**

Cumulative Score, X Quizzes:

_____ **Points**

Seeing through brick walls is a talent of the fictional Superman. But seeing through the walls of the heart is a power of the true God. What do you know about His "X-Ray Vision"?

Answers on next page.

100 What son did King David tell, "The Lord searches every heart and understands every motive"?

200 What troublemaking religious leaders—accusing Jesus of casting out demons by the prince of demons—had their thoughts read by Jesus?

300 What great prophet heard God say, "Man looks at the outward appearance, but the Lord looks at the heart"?

400 What did Jesus say God would do for the believers He sees secretly giving to the needy?

500 What "el"oquent friend of Job proclaimed God's complete knowledge, saying, "There is no dark place. . . where evildoers can hide"?

X-Ray
Vision answers

100	Solomon (1 Chronicles 28:2–10)
200	Pharisees (Matthew 12:22–28)
300	Samuel (1 Samuel 16:7)
400	reward them (Matthew 6:3–4)
500	Elihu (Job 34:1–22)

Your Score for This Quiz:

_____ Points

Total Score, X Quizzes:

_____ Points

Risk It!

X Marks the Spot

You've gotten through the *X* quizzes. . .and now you'll *Risk It!* How does this "X Marks the Spot" category sound to you? Think over how much of your total score on the *X* quizzes you want to risk on the one question following. If you answer correctly, you add the amount you risked to your total *X* quiz score. . .if you answer incorrectly, you *subtract* the amount you risked. Have a figure in mind? Mark down the amount you're willing to risk, and we'll unveil the question. . . .

Your Total Score, X Quizzes:

_____ Points

Your Risk It! Amount:

_____ Points

In a parable describing the kingdom of heaven, where did Jesus say a man found a hidden treasure?

Answer on next page.

Risk It! answer

in a field (Matthew 13:44)

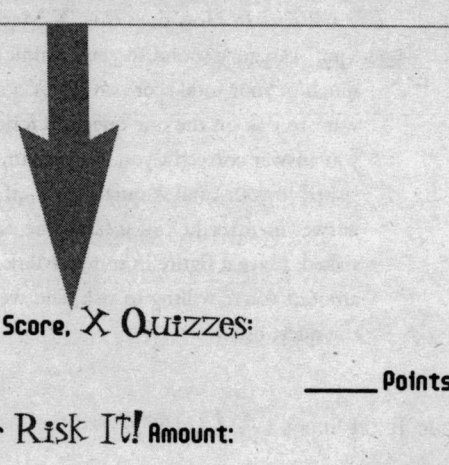

Your Total Score, X Quizzes:

_____ **Points**

+ or – Your Risk It! Amount:

_____ **Points**

Running Total (A through H Quizzes):

_____ **Points**

Yachtsmen

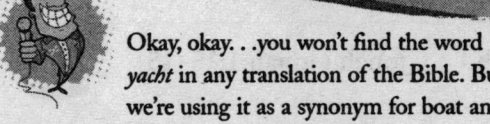

Okay, okay. . .you won't find the word *yacht* in any translation of the Bible. But we're using it as a synonym for boat and asking you to tell us about the sailors of Scripture.

Answers on next page.

100 What wayward prophet was thrown overboard by pagan sailors frightened by a violent storm at sea?

200 What alliterative brothers were in a boat when Jesus called them to be His disciples?

300 What was Jesus doing in a boat immediately before calming a storm that terrified His disciples?

400 What wise and wealthy king, who built God's first temple, also built ships on the Red Sea?

500 What island's people welcomed the apostle Paul and 275 other people after their ship broke apart in the Adriatic Sea?

Yachtsmen answers

100	Jonah (Jonah 1:13–15)
200	James and John (Matthew 4:21–22)
300	sleeping (Luke 8:22–25)
400	Solomon (1 Kings 9:26–28)
500	Malta, or Melita (Acts 27:37–28:2)

Your Score for This Quiz:

_____ Points

Yellow-Bellies

That's an Old West term for "cowards"—
and there were a few of them in the Bible.
Tell us what you remember about these.

Answers on next page.

100 How many times during Jesus' arrest and trial did Simon Peter deny he knew the Lord?

200 What did the terrified disciples think they were seeing when Jesus walked across the water to their boat?

300 What wicked queen threatened the life of the prophet Elijah, causing him to pray to God that he would die?

400 What conspiring son of King David caused his father to flee for his life from Jerusalem?

500 What Israelite leader, preparing for battle against the Midianites, saw twenty-two thousand warriors—more than two-thirds of his army—desert when given the chance?

Yellow-Bellies
answers

100	three (Luke 22:54–62)
200	a ghost, or spirit (Matthew 14:22–27)
300	Jezebel (1 Kings 19:1–4)
400	Absalom (2 Samuel 15:13–37)
500	Gideon (Judges 7:1–3)

Your Score for This Quiz:

_____ Points

Cumulative Score, Y Quizzes:

_____ Points

Yokes

Ha ha. . .the yoke's on you! Yeah, we know that's a bad pun, but there are yokes in the Bible that belong on people, as well as animals. What can you recall about them?

Answers on next page.

100   How did Jesus describe the yoke He places on His followers?

200   What color of heifer—which had never worn a yoke—were Moses and Aaron instructed to sacrifice?

300   What kind of yoking did the apostle Paul warn the church at Corinth about?

400   What Old Testament prophet, who called himself "a child," wore a wooden yoke as an object lesson?

500   What king, the son of Solomon, threatened to place his subjects under a heavy yoke—and caused many of the tribes of Israel to rebel?

Yokes answers

100	easy (Matthew 11:28–30)
200	red (Numbers 19:1–5)
300	with unbelievers, or unequal (2 Corinthians 6:14)
400	Jeremiah (Jeremiah 1:6, 28:12–14)
500	Rehoboam (1 Kings 12:1–19)

Your Score for This Quiz:

_____ Points

Cumulative Score, Y Quizzes:

_____ Points

Young People

You have to be thirty-five to become president of the United States. But you can serve the Lord at any age. What do you know about these five young people of the Bible?

Answers on next page.

100 What instrument did the young David play to soothe the troubled spirit of King Saul?

200 What boy, destined to become a great prophet of Israel, ministered in the temple under the priest Eli?

300 How old was the boy Jesus when He amazed people in the temple with His spiritual insights?

400 What young king removed all the mediums and spiritists from Judah, as required in the book of the law found by his priest, Hilkiah?

500 What young relative of Paul discovered and reported a plot to kill the apostle in Jerusalem?

Young People answers

100	harp (1 Samuel 16:18–19)
200	Samuel (1 Samuel 3:1)
300	twelve (Luke 2:41–52)
400	Josiah (2 Kings 22:1–8, 23:24–25)
500	his nephew, or sister's son (Acts 23:12–22)

Your Score for This Quiz:

_____ **Points**

Total Score, Y Quizzes:

_____ **Points**

Risk It!

Yearly Things

It's time again to *Risk It!*—this time, for your score on the four *Y* quizzes. We're talking about yearly things in the Bible. Decide how much of your total score on the *Y* quizzes you want to risk on the one question following. If you answer correctly, you add the amount you risked to your total *Y* quiz score. . .if you answer incorrectly, you *subtract* the amount you risked. Are you ready? Jot down the amount you're willing to risk, and we'll unveil the question. . . .

Your Total Score, Y Quizzes:

_____ Points

Your Risk It! Amount:

_____ Points

What annual celebration was instituted to commemorate the Jews' victory over their enemies in Queen Esther's time?

Answer on next page.

Risk It! answer

> Purim (Esther 9:20–28)

Your Total Score, Y Quizzes:

_____ **Points**

+ or – Your Risk It! Amount:

_____ **Points**

Running Total (A through Y Quizzes):

_____ **Points**

Zacchaeus

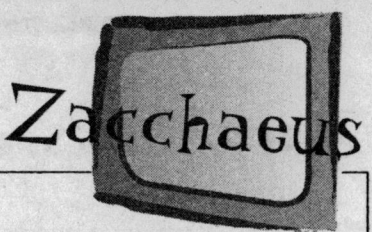

If you know the Sunday school song about Zacchaeus, you might want to sing it to yourself. . . . It'll probably help you answer some of these questions!

Answers on next page.

100 What physical characteristic initially hindered Zacchaeus from seeing Jesus?

200 What was Zacchaeus's line of work?

300 What derogatory name did the crowd call Zacchaeus when Jesus visited his home?

400 What town was home to Zacchaeus?

500 How much did Zacchaeus promise to pay back to anyone he had cheated?

Zacchaeus answers

100	shortness (Luke 19:3)
200	tax collector, or publican (Luke 19:2)
300	"a sinner" (Luke 19:7)
400	Jericho (Luke 19:1, 5–6)
500	four times the amount (Luke 19:8)

Your Score for This Quiz:

_____ Points

Zechariah Who?

Like Michael or Jason today, Zechariah was a very popular name in Bible times. Your job in this quiz is to sort out which Zechariah is which.

Answers on next page.

100 What famed evangelist was born to a priest named Zechariah?

200 At what place of worship was Zechariah, the son of the high priest Jehoiada, stoned to death for condemning Judah's idolatry?

300 What violent act ended the reign of the evil King Zechariah of Israel only six months after he took power?

400 What structure in Jerusalem did a certain Zechariah, son of Jonathan, help Nehemiah dedicate?

500 What type of tree surrounded a man on a red horse in a vision of the prophet Zechariah?

261

Zechariah Who? answers

100	John the Baptist (Luke 1:57–60)
200	the temple (2 Chronicles 24:17–22)
300	assassination (2 Kings 15:8–10)
400	the wall (Nehemiah 12:27–37)
500	myrtle (Zechariah 1:7–8)

Your Score for This Quiz:

_____ Points

Cumulative Score, Z Quizzes:

_____ Points

Z Inside

Well, what better clue can we give you than that? Every answer in this quiz will include a *Z* somewhere inside.

Answers on next page.

100 What town in Galilee was the boyhood home of Jesus?

200 What word described the crowd's response when Jesus used His authority to drive out evil spirits?

300 What Philistine city's name is still heard in the news today, often with the word "strip"?

400 What "prince of demons" did Pharisees accuse Jesus of using to cast out demons?

500 What town, along with Bethsaida, did not repent when Jesus performed miracles there and thus received a pronouncement of woe?

Z Inside answers

100	Nazareth (Matthew 2:19–23)
200	amazed (Mark 1:23–27)
300	Gaza (2 Kings 18:8)
400	Beelzebub (Mark 3:22)
500	Korazin, or Chorazin (Matthew 11:20–21)

Your Score for This Quiz:

_____ Points

Cumulative Score, Z Quizzes:

_____ Points

A classic hymn says that "glorious things of thee are spoken, Zion, city of our God." What do you know about this important place?

Answers on next page.

100 What great king of Israel captured the fortress of Zion from mocking Jebusites?

200 What happy musical compositions of Zion did the psalmist remember longingly "by the rivers of Babylon"?

300 What important religious artifact was brought from Zion to the new temple built by Solomon?

400 What kind of stone, according to the apostle Paul, did God lay in Zion?

500 How many of those "redeemed from the earth" stood with the Lamb on Mount Zion in John's Revelation?

Zion answers

100	David (2 Samuel 5:6–8)
200	songs (Psalm 137:1–3)
300	the ark of the covenant (1 Kings 8:1–5)
400	stumbling (Romans 9:32–33)
500	144,000 (Revelation 14:1–3)

Your Score for This Quiz:

_____ Points

Total Score, Z Quizzes:

_____ Points

Risk It!

Zealous People

Well, the four Z quizzes are now in the books. . . and it's your final opportunity to *Risk It!* How does a category on "Zealous People" sound? Consider how much of your total score on the Z quizzes you want to risk on the one question to follow. If you answer correctly, you add the amount you risked to your total Z quiz score. . .if you answer incorrectly, you *subtract* the amount you risked. Are you ready? Mark down the amount you're willing to risk, and we'll unveil the question. . . .

Your Total Score, Z Quizzes:

_____ Points

Your Risk It! Amount:

_____ Points

What was the first name of the apostle known as "the zealot" or "Zelotes"?

Answer on next page.

Risk It! answer

Simon (Luke 6:12–16)

Your Total Score, Z Quizzes:

_____ Points

+ or – Your Risk It! Amount:

_____ Points

Grand Total (A through Z Quizzes):

_____ Points

What's a perfect score in A to Z Bible Trivia? If you answered every question correctly and successfully risked your total score for every letter of the alphabet, you'd have 312,000 points! So, how'd you do?

LIKE BIBLE TRIVIA?

Then check out these great books from Barbour Publishing!

The Bible Detective by Carol Smith
Solve mysteries posed by a mixed-up story using biblical characters, places, and quotations.
> ISBN 1-57748-838-5/Paperback/224 pages/$2.97

My Final Answer by Paul Kent
Thirty separate quizzes feature twelve multiple-choice questions each—and the questions get progressively harder!
> ISBN 1-58660-030-3/Paperback/256 pages/$2.97

Bible IQ by Rayburn Ray
One hundred sections of ten questions each—and a systematic scoring system to tell you just how well you did.
> ISBN 1-57748-837-7/Paperback/256 pages/$2.97

Test Your Bible Knowledge by Carl Shoup
Over 1,400 multiple-choice questions to test your mettle, tickle your funny bone, and tantalize your intellect.
> ISBN 1-55748-541-0/Paperback/224 pages/$2.97

Fun Facts About the Bible by Robyn Martins
Challenging and intriguing Bible trivia—expect some of the answers to surprise you!
> ISBN 1-55748-897-5/Paperback/256 pages/$2.97

Available wherever books are sold.
Or order from:

Barbour Publishing, Inc.
P.O. Box 719
Uhrichsville, OH 44683
www.barbourbooks.com

If you order by mail add $2.00 to your order for shipping.
Prices subject to change without notice.